GOLDEN YEARS, GOLDEN PLATES

Golden Years, Golden Plates

Eating Well After 50

B. VINCENT

QuantumQuill Press

CONTENTS

Chapter 1: Introduction — 1

Chapter 2: Understanding Aging and Nutrition — 9

Chapter 3: Building a Foundation: The Basics of Healthy Eating — 18

Chapter 4: Nutritional Needs for Older Adults — 24

Chapter 5: The Mediterranean Diet: A Blueprint for Healthy Aging — 32

Chapter 6: Cooking for One or Two — 40

Chapter 7: Eating Out: Navigating Restaurants and Social Gatherings — 49

Chapter 8: Managing Special Dietary Needs — 58

9	Chapter 9: Maintaining a Healthy Weight and Body Composition	68
10	Chapter 10: Mindful Eating and Emotional Health	78
11	Chapter 11: Staying Hydrated: The Importance of Water and Fluid Intake	87
12	Chapter 12: Planning for the Future: Nutrition and Longevity	96
13	Chapter 13: Conclusion	105

Copyright © 2024 by B. Vincent

All rights reserved. No part of this book may be reproduced in any manner whatsoever without written permission except in the case of brief quotations embodied in critical articles and reviews.

First Printing, 2024

| 1 |

Chapter 1: Introduction

After 50, the Meaning of Smart Dieting

It is difficult to exaggerate the significance of sticking to a solid and even eating routine as one methodology for their brilliant years. The job of sustenance in deciding the course of our wellbeing as we age is pivotal, as it influences our imperativeness, versatility, and general condition. Starting with this segment, we will examine the justifications for why keeping a solid eating routine after the age of 50 isn't just suggested but urgent for making progress from now on.

In a time when food served exclusively as a wellspring of food or joy, its job has developed into a major part of our wellbeing methodology as we face the complexities of maturing. Over the long haul, the human body encounters a huge number of changes, remembering vaccinations for digestion and enhancements in the effectiveness of supplement retention. It is basic to fathom these nuances of physiology to redo our dietary choices to accommodate the changing necessities of our bodies.

By coordinating observational proof with engaging accounts, we look at the significant impact that sustenance can have on our general wellbeing. The upsides of keeping a nutritious eating routine rise above the limits of the feasting region, as they increase mental capability and safeguard against persistent infections. An assessment of the latest epidemiological information and examination discoveries uncovers the undeniable connection between today's dietary examples and the future.

Besides, we should defy the brutal reality of maturing straightforwardly, perceiving the unmistakable obstructions and susceptibilities that are innate to this period of presence. Our nourishing necessities likewise develop with the body, which highlights the significance of embracing a proactive position towards dietary preparation and the board. We intend to expose pervasive deceptions relating to sustenance and maturing through the utilization of proof-based thinking and useful insight.

By using individual stories and substantial occasions from the real world, we exhibit the significant effect that embracing nutritious dietary practices can have in the later phases of life. We gain important direction from specialists and people who have effectively explored the complicated scene of dietary changes; we look for insight from the individuals who have had to deal with this excursion already. Their encounters act as motivational updates that one can constantly start an extraordinary way toward further developed wellbeing and essentialness.

In a general sense, this starting section can be an enthusiastic allure, convincing perusers to recognize the significant impact that legitimate nourishment can have on their later years. It lays out an establishment for ensuing examinations concerning the topic, invigorating curiosity and stimulus to give priority to one's wellbeing and, in general, government assistance. Allow us to mutually embrace the extraordinary capability of nutritious eating as we start this undertaking and lay out a way towards a more brilliant and hopeful future during our brilliant years.

Grasping the Methods Involved in Maturing

Maturing is an inborn and inescapable part that is unpredictably woven into the texture of our being. As we progress as the years progress, our bodies experience a progression of mind-boggling changes, every one of which lastingly affects our general wellbeing and condition. Inside this fragment, we begin an investigation of the maturing system, diving into its puzzling nature and the significant consequences it has on our wholesome prerequisites.

The investigation is predicated on a perception of the physiological changes that happen with age. Our bodies go through an exceptional development over the long haul, described by a steady diminishing in metabolic rate and a fading effectiveness in supplement retention. We broadly inspect the intricacies of these changes, explaining the hidden systems that administer our developing nourishing necessities.

The idea of supplement thickness, which expresses that as we age, our bodies require a more prominent amount of supplements per calorie to keep up with ideal wellbeing, is fundamental to this conversation. It is an unforgiving truth that supplement deficiencies become more pervasive as one ages, introducing a significant risk to general wellbeing. Outfitted with this data, we empower perusers to decisively decide their food utilization, consequently ensuring that they satisfy the steadily changing necessities of their bodies.

Besides, we explore the impacts of maturing on the guidelines of hunger, taste insight, and food inclinations, recognizing the multifaceted connection between physiological changes and dietary practices. A huge number of elements, remembering variances for chemical levels and the slow decay of taste buds, are uncovered to affect the manner in which people see and draw in with food as they age.

Nonetheless, notwithstanding these hindrances, we find guts and opportunity. Acquiring information on the complexities of the maturing system gives significant knowledge into how one can effectively advance their wellbeing and imperativeness by means of dietary decisions. We foster a comprehension of the significance of balance by choosing food sources that are plentiful in supplements that support our actual prosperity as well as elevate our psychological state.

On a very basic level, this section has the capability of directing light, revealing insight into the direction towards achieving top wellbeing and health during our later years. Through the investigation of the mysteries encompassing the maturing system, we empower perusers to apply organization to their dietary destiny, in this manner laying out a direction toward power, guts, and life span. Let us continue with our endeavor to access the quest for a more dynamic and cognizant future, perceiving the significant effect that information can have on us.

Going up against misrepresentations and misguided judgments

In the midst of the far-reaching domain of nourishment, there is a bounty of paradoxes and false impressions that darken the direction towards achieving top wellbeing. Chasing a sound eating regimen during advanced age, it is urgent to recognize reality and fiction to get our personalities free from the deception that takes steps to darken our judgment. During this section, we try to expose the paradoxes and misconceptions related to nourishment and maturing by utilizing commonsense information and proof-based thinking.

A predominant error inside the field of nourishment is the conviction that propelling age kills the capacity to change one's dietary examples. As one ages, it is generally accepted that inclinations set and the ability to embrace more wellbeing-conscious dietary propensities decreases. Be that as it may, nothing could be further from reality than this. Various examinations have shown that individuals across all age groups display an extraordinary limit with regards to improvement and change, making them fit for laying out original schedules and embracing better approaches to everyday life.

An extra-pervasive paradox is the thought that sticking to a solid eating regimen involves difficulty and penance, comprising a perpetual weariness with boring and unacceptable food. Nonetheless, nothing could be further from reality than this. Sticking to a sound eating routine doesn't involve limits but instead appreciation—an upbeat festival of the sustaining supplements and distinctive flavors that nature gives. By taking on a fluctuating choice of entire food sources that are bountiful in variety, flavor, and surface, we can enjoy the delights of the culinary domain while at the same time giving interior sustenance to our bodies.

Nonetheless, amidst a whirlwind of inconsistent messages, it very well may be hard to recognize reality and fiction. Consistently, we are immersed in thrilling titles, trend diets, and marvel supplements that have the way to timeless youth and essentialness. Notwithstanding, an immortal truth stays covered underneath the glistening outside of promoting misrepresentation: great wellbeing can't be accomplished in a rush. Veritable prosperity is laid out upon a bedrock of adjusted sustenance, predictable commitment to active work, and the act of care—fundamental precepts that have withstood everyday hardship.

Generally, this fragment has the potential to be an ardent allure, convincing perusers to fundamentally look at the predominant standards and challenge the deceptions and false impressions that have generally overwhelmed our understanding of sustenance. Through the reception of an outlook portrayed by interest and knowing judgment, people can acquire the capacity to settle on instructed choices concerning their wellbeing and, generally, government assistance, freed from the imperatives forced by misleading data and wrong convictions. As we progress along our way, may we boldly forsake any questions and brazenly embrace reality, consequently laying out a direction towards a future portrayed by further developed wellbeing and essentialness.

Laying out Down-to-Earth Assumptions

Inside the space of wellbeing and sustenance, the quest for ideal health is often portrayed as a direct direction—aa calculated movement that rules out deviations or hindrances. Be that as it may, this glorified record disregards the mind-boggling intricacies of the human condition, in which progression regularly follows a non-straight direction and accomplishment is resolved not by the absence of hindrances but rather by our ability to conquer them. Inside this portion, we begin an investigation to rearrange our expectations, perceiving the worth of flaws while laying out feasible targets that honor the uniqueness of every individual's way.

The core of this talk is the affirmation that certifiable prosperity is certainly not a decent endpoint, but rather a constant movement—aa dynamic and never-endingly taking a different path of improvement and reflection. As opposed to the paradox of a generally material eating routine that ensures ideal wellbeing and bliss, we reject the idea of the "great" diet and embrace the thought of bio-uniqueness, which holds that each individual has particular wholesome necessities and tendencies impacted by hereditary qualities, way of life, and environmental elements.

Moreover, we perceive the characteristic intricacies and unusualness that follow in the undertaking to accomplish ideal wellbeing and health. There are various difficulties that take steps to block our progress, going from the appeal of contemporary food sources to the requests of cultural standards. In any case, amidst turmoil and flightiness, people find solace in the limit with respect to versatility—the ability to recuperate from hindrances and progress steadily—all things being equal.

The idea of self-sympathy, which involves treating oneself with thoughtfulness and understanding, especially during times of difficulty or misery, is central to this talk. We reject the idea of compulsiveness, which involves an unflinching mission for an unattainable norm, and, on second thought, value the charm of blemish—the obfuscated, imperfect, and stunningly human course of creating oneself and advancing.

Generally, this section serves as a motivation, revealing insight into the direction towards a more salubrious and fulfilling presence—one that isn't predicated on unrealistic norms or resolute guidelines, but rather on a bold soul, mettle, and self-sympathy. By taking on a hopeful standpoint and perceiving the worth of blemishes, we can cultivate a feeling of control and self-assurance with respect to our physical and emotional well-being, in this manner laying out a direction towards an additional, promising, and dynamic future. As we progress along our way, let us gradually free ourselves from the imperatives of hairsplitting and earnestly embrace the significant effect that self-empathy can have.

A Summary of the Book

Considering our inevitable embarkation on this significant endeavor towards ideal wellbeing and prosperity during our brilliant years, it is important that we procure an extensive understanding of the direction that looks for us. Inside this closing piece of the early part, we present an exhaustive outline of the way we are going to follow, outfitting a navigational device that will guide us through the plentiful exhibit of subjects and understandings that exist in the pages of this scholarly work.

Our examination begins with a far-reaching investigation of the physiological changes that happen during the maturing system, in this way enlightening the mind-boggling connection between sustenance and maturing. In this way, an investigation of the errors and false impressions that regularly darken our appreciation of sustenance follows, giving perusers the essential assets to separate veracity from misrepresentation inside the complex domain of dietary proposals.

Accordingly, we address the trouble of laying out commonsense expectations, perceiving the characteristic complexities and flightiness that involve the undertaking to accomplish ideal wellbeing and health. By taking on an outlook fixated on self-empathy and versatility, we empower perusers to see the value in the intrinsic worth of defects and defy the difficulties they will face with levelheadedness and reflection.

When solid groundwork has been laid out, we dive into the functional contemplations of maintaining a sound eating regimen in our later years. In this distribution, we dig into the nourishing necessities of the old and look at the benefits of the Mediterranean eating routine as a system for sound maturing. To assist perusers in coordinating sustaining food sources into their regular schedules, we provide functional guidance, methodologies, and recipes.

Our excursion, in any case, doesn't end there. It is recognized that veritable prosperity envelops all features of our physical, mental, and profound wellbeing, notwithstanding sustenance. In quest for this goal, we dig into the meaning of close-to-home wellbeing, actual work, careful eating, and hydration, subsequently giving complete ways to deal with encouraging a dynamic and fulfilling presence during our later years.

On a very basic level, this book functions as a comprehensive manual—aa friendship all through the quest for top wellbeing and health during the later years. By incorporating logical information, practical direction, and genuine inspiration, we empower perusers to proactively decide their wellbeing direction, gradually executing feeding choices. As we progress all in all, may we sincerely take on the outlook-changing capability of nutritious dietary practices and establish the groundwork for a more glowing and lively future during our brilliant years.

| 2 |

Chapter 2: Understanding Aging and Nutrition

Alterations to Physiology with Maturing

With the movement of time and the collection of years, the human body encounters an unprecedented grouping of changes, every one of which affects our general prosperity and strength. Inside this portion, we start an examination concerning the intricacies innate in the maturing system, diving into the physiological changes that impact our dietary necessities and examples of eating as we get older.

Figuring out digestion—aa mind-boggling framework of biochemical cycles that supply energy to the body and control energy consumption—is integral to this conversation. Our metabolic rate normally decelerates with age, bringing about a dynamic decrease in energy requests and a raised vulnerability to weight gain and metabolic issues. We investigate the fundamental systems of this metabolic deceleration, subsequently enlightening the components that contribute to modifications in body synthesis and energy offset related to maturing.

Moreover, we are defied by the awkward truth that absorption decline is an intrinsic part of the maturing system and can disable the use and osmosis of supplements from food. We look at the assorted scope of results that can emerge from age-related changes in stomach-related capability, including modified gastrointestinal motility and diminished stomach corrosive discharge, which can affect dietary status and overall wellbeing. By coordinating logical information with practical direction, we empower perusers to procure information that illuminates their dietary choices and supplement utilization, consequently ensuring that they satisfy the advancing prerequisites of their bodies as they progress in age.

In any case, in spite of these hindrances, we find strength and opportunity. By procuring information about the intricacies related to the maturing system, we can foster a proactive way to deal with upgrading our wellbeing and imperativeness through dietary means. We foster a comprehension of the significance of control by choosing food sources that are bountiful in supplements that support our actual prosperity as well as elevate our psychological state.

On a very basic level, this fragment serves as a foundation for our journey for the greatest wellbeing and health in our later years. Through the investigation of the puzzles encompassing the maturing system, we empower perusers to apply organization to their dietary destiny, in this way laying out a direction toward power, grit, and life span. Allow us to additionally examine the extraordinary capability of information and start an excursion towards a future characterized by further developed wellbeing and imperativeness.

Fundamental Supplements for the Older

Our bodies require an agreeable structure of supplements to work at their most elevated limit, with every supplement satisfying a fundamental capability in advancing our wellbeing and in general government assistance. As one methodologies their brilliant years, the meaning of furnishing their bodies with these major structural blocks turns out to be progressively obvious. This part gives an inside-and-out investigation of the nourishing prerequisites of people who are 50 years old or older. It enlightens the fundamental supplements that are basic for cultivating life span and strength.

As of now, our examination is centered around calcium, which is central to keeping up with solid bones and skeletal honesty. Because of the increased risk of osteoporosis and bone cracks with age, it is essential to consume adequate calcium to safeguard powerful and solid bones. In this article, we investigate the ideal day-to-day calcium utilization for the old populace and give pragmatic ideas for coordinating calcium-rich food sources into our everyday practice, including dairy items, verdant greens, and strengthened refreshments.

Moreover, we underscore the meaning of vitamin D, a fundamental supplement that is instrumental in both the osmosis of calcium and the digestion of bone. With age, the body's capacity to create vitamin D from daylight reduces, requiring supplementation or dietary admission of this supplement. In this article, we talk about the ideal everyday vitamin D utilization for more seasoned adults. Furthermore, we offer functional counsel on the most proficient method to integrate vitamin D-rich food varieties into our eating routine, including greasy salmon, eggs, and braced dairy items, and guarantee satisfactory openness to daylight.

Notwithstanding calcium and vitamin D, we currently shift our concentration to fiber, a fundamental dietary component that has broad ramifications for both stomach-related wellbeing and general government assistance. Obstruction and gastrointestinal problems become more common with age; thus, it is indispensable to devour fiber-rich food sources, including natural products, vegetables, entire grains, and vegetables, to help stomach-related capability and advance routineness. As well as discussing the recommended everyday fiber utilization for more seasoned people, we investigate sober-minded ways to deal with coordinating food sources abundant in fiber into our schedules and improving stomach-related prosperity.

Besides, we dive into the meaning of hydration—aa principal part of all encompassing wellbeing and government assistance that expects a logically basic nature with propelling age. Because of the way that parchedness can bring about mental debilitation, urinary tract diseases, and kidney stones, among others, keeping a predictable liquid utilization over the course of the day is basic. In this talk, we envelop useful ideas for keeping up with hydration and coordinating hydrating food varieties and drinks into our day-to-day routine, including water-rich vegetables, natural products, and home-grown teas, notwithstanding the day-to-day liquid admission suggestion for senior adults.

In a general sense, this portion can be an aid for crossing the multifaceted scene of nourishing requirements during the later phases of life. By acquiring a perception of the interesting prerequisites of the human body as it ages, we can empower ourselves to go with the instructed choices in regards to our dietary practices and economically improve our wellbeing and, generally speaking, prosperity. Allow us to drive forward in our undertakings while perceiving the significant effect that food can have on an improved and more unique future.

Regular medical problems Connected to the Maturing System

Over the long haul, as we explore the course of our lives, we definitely stand up to a large number of medical problems that expand in pervasiveness as we age. These difficulties, going from the unnoticeable signs of osteoporosis to the disturbing outcomes of coronary illness and mental weakening, piercingly highlight our mortality and the unsafe idea of the human condition. This part gives an investigation of the common medical problems that emerge with the maturing system, enlightening the perplexing connection among sustenance and by and large wellbeing during the later long stretches of life.

One of the essential subjects of examination is osteoporosis, an intangible misdirection that subverts skeletal strength and bone thickness, leaving people powerless to break and fall. The probability of creating osteoporosis increases with age; in this manner, it is basic to give priority to bone wellbeing by carrying out a routine that incorporates weight-bearing activity, dietary changes, and way of life changes. This study investigates the meaning of calcium, vitamin D, and other imperative supplements in advancing bone wellbeing. It gives significant suggestions for preventing osteoporosis and keeping up with the honesty of the skeleton.

Related to osteoporosis, we likewise face the considerable danger of cardiovascular illness—an indistinct death that quickly asserts lives—an extra concern. The risk of cardiovascular sickness increases with age because of an intersection of hereditary defenselessness, way of life decisions, and previous ailments. The significance of a heart-solid eating routine rich in organic products, vegetables, entire grains, lean proteins, and sound lipids is underlined as we look at the role of diet in the counteraction and the executives of cardiovascular sickness. We deliberated on dietary interventions upheld by logical proof, including the Mediterranean eating routine, the Run diet, and the plant-based diet. We additionally give commonsense ideas for coordinating heart-healthy food varieties into our regular day-to-day existences.

Moreover, mental degradation—aa slow and reliable weakening of memory, cognizance, and chief capability—presents a tricky risk that can possibly deny us our independence and healthy identity. Mental deterioration turns out to be more plausible with advancing age; in this way, it is basic to integrate into our regular routines rehearses that advance cerebrum wellbeing and mental capability. An assessment is directed at the effect of nourishment on mental wellbeing, with an emphasis on the benefits that omega-3 unsaturated fats, cell-reinforcement-rich food varieties, and different supplements add to mind capability. By giving practical ways to deal with coordinating mind-upgrading food varieties into one's dietary and way of life decisions, we empower perusers to take on a proactive position in their endeavors to shield mental capability and support smartness all through the maturing system.

On a very basic level, this section provides a strong indication of the huge impact that nourishment can have on the course of our maturing wellbeing. Through an understanding of the common medical problems that concur with the maturing system and the meaning of diet in lessening their expected perils, we can empower ourselves to accept authority over our wellbeing direction and welcome a future overflowing with energy, guts, and health. In our continuous undertakings, may we think about the bits of knowledge acquired from past encounters and lay out a way towards a seriously encouraging and wellbeing-conscious future during our brilliant years.

The Impact of Maturing on Craving and Taste Insight

In the midst of the organization of tactile discernments that comprise the human condition, gustation and appetite act as corresponding underpinnings of satisfaction and sustenance. Nonetheless, as one explores the intricate labyrinth of presence, preferences and hungers habitually experience nuanced changes and advancements, affected by the relentless movement of time. This part digs into the impacts of maturing on the guidelines of hunger, flavor discernment, and food inclinations, revealing insight into the perplexing connection between changes related to maturing and dietary examples later on.

Taste insight, a tangible wonder that empowers us to savor the multitudinous flavors and surfaces of the culinary world, is integral to our examination. With the movement old enough, the number and responsiveness of taste buds logically lessen, bringing about a weakening of the tactile orchestra of taste. The previously mentioned decrease in gustatory discernment might bring about a compromised deference for surfaces and flavors, in this manner entangling the errand of getting satisfaction from food. An investigation of the physiological systems that underlie changes in taste discernment related to maturing gives significant bits of knowledge into the possible results of these progressions on dietary examples and wholesome utilization.

Besides, we are faced with the mind-boggling difficulties of craving guidelines, which oversee our dietary patterns and dietary utilization through a sensitive dance among yearning and satiety. The mind-boggling exchange of chemicals and synapses that oversee craving bit by bit decays with age, bringing about adjustments to the signs of yearning and satiety. Such conditions might prompt changes in eating ways of behaving; certain individuals might notice a decrease in their cravings, while others might fight with unreasonable food utilization or close-to-home eating. This study looks at the different components that contribute to modifications in craving guidelines related to maturing and gives significant suggestions for protecting a sound harmony among yearning and satiety.

Notwithstanding craving guidelines and taste discernment, food inclinations are a complicated transaction of physiological variables, social impacts, and individual encounters that influence our dietary choices and dietary patterns. Geriatricians might encounter steady adjustments in their dietary inclinations because of elements like changed taste discernment, hunger guidelines, and wholesome prerequisites. We give pragmatic guidance on the most proficient method to answer age-related changes in food inclinations, which can affect dietary propensities and wholesome admission. Thusly, we guarantee that one keeps a reasonable and supportive eating regimen.

In a general sense, this portion is a strong sign of the complicated exchange between dietary examples in later life and age-related changes. By gaining information in regards to the impacts of maturing on taste discernment, hunger guidelines, and food inclinations, people can prepare themselves to settle on all-around informed choices in regards to their dietary practices and nutrient utilization. This will ensure that they will never-endingly track down happiness and sustenance in the gastronomic delights of their presence. Allow us to further our investigation by valuing the delights of the ongoing second and embracing the significant effect that careful eating can have during our later years.

Social and mental elements that influence sustenance in the old

The mental and social encounters of people are complicatedly interlaced with the dietary parts that contain the perplexing embroidery of human life. As one advances through their brilliant years, these interconnected variables have a continuously more noteworthy impact on their dietary examples, nourishing utilization, and general condition of wellbeing. This segment digs into the mental and social determinants that influence nourishment during the maturing system, giving knowledge into the complicated elements that exist between the human brain, actual body, and general climate.

Key to our examination is the unavoidable issue of dejection, which is an incognito pestilence that denies a great many senior residents overall significant cooperation, everyday encouragement, and social association. The gamble of dejection rises with propelling age, moved by different elements including retirement, mourning, and actual crippling. This study investigates the critical impact of forlornness on dietary ways of behaving and nourishing admission, underscoring the relationship between people's friendly disconnection and horrible health outcomes. By coordinating experimental proof with narrative proof, we shed light on the meaning of developing social bonds and emotionally supportive networks as a way to energize nutritious dietary practices and comprehensive government assistance during the later, longer periods of life.

Besides, we are defied by the presence of despair, a dismal cloud that can possibly darken the delights of presence and reduce the craving for food. Wretchedness turns out to be more prevalent with advancing age and takes a chance with factors incorporating persistent sickness, incapacity, and social separation. An assessment is led into the perplexing connection amongst sustenance and discouragement, with an accentuation on the manners by which vacillations in effect and state of mind can impact dietary examples and the amount of supplements consumed. Our association gives sober-minded ways to deal with overseeing sorrow and improving mental prosperity by means of dietary alterations, with an emphasis on the criticality of counseling psychological wellness suppliers and medical services experts for help.

Notwithstanding despondency and depression, financial variables, which can block access to nutritious food and damage endeavors to maintain a sound eating regimen, are likewise deserving of thought. Expanding monetary uncertainty improves the probability that a single person will not be able to manage the cost of nutritious food or use fundamental administrations like medical services and transportation. This study analyzes the impact of financial status on dietary choices and healthful admission. It gives significant guidance on overcoming impediments to keeping a sound eating routine and making reasonable, sustaining food decisions.

This part successfully highlights the significant interdependencies that exist among the brain, body, and climate, which essentially impact our future healthful encounters. Through an understanding of the mental and social determinants that influence nourishment, we can furnish ourselves with the capacity to stand up to the hidden reasons for troublesome dietary practices and promote comprehensive health during our later years. As we progress along our way, may we encourage an increased cognizance in regards to the relationship of our prosperity and acknowledge the significant impact that shared commitment, profound help, and social connection have on sustaining our erudite, physical, and otherworldly creatures.

| 3 |

Chapter 3: Building a Foundation: The Basics of Healthy Eating

The groundwork of a fair eating regimen

Inside the perplexing texture of nourishment, a sound eating regimen is predicated on the amicable harmony of supplement-rich staples that give food to the body and keep up with general wellbeing. This part starts an investigation of the primary precepts of an even eating regimen, coordinating perusers towards a more significant understanding of the food varieties that support energy and energize old age.

The pith of our examination revolves around the idea of assortment—the enhancing part of our dietary collection that confers a different exhibit of tastes, surfaces, and supplements. A reasonable eating regimen includes a wide assortment of food sources addressing every food class, consequently providing a broad exhibit of fundamental supplements that advance by and large wellbeing and health. The meaning of coordinating organic products, vegetables, entire grains, lean proteins, and solid lipids into our everyday eating regimens is inspected, with an accentuation on the unmistakable nourishing benefits related to every food classification.

Moreover, we look at the meaning of piece control in support of a nutritious eating regimen, putting specific accentuation on the need to notice the body's signs of hunger and satiety. Extent control is pivotal for forestalling gorging and keeping a sound load in a general public where voracious smorgasbords and super-sized segments captivate us every step of the way. Viable systems for parceling feasts and rewards are given, including the execution of careful eating methods, the usage of more modest plates, and the estimation of serving sizes.

The thought of careful eating, which urges us to foster an uplifted consciousness of our food choices, eating designs, and real signs, is major to our talk. Dialing back, relishing every significant piece, and guiding one's focus toward the substantial vibes of craving, totality, and fulfillment comprise careful eating. One can foster a more certain impression of food and improve one's general wellbeing by deliberately going to substantial signals and devouring intentionally.

In a general sense, this section has the capability of serving as a navigational signal, revealing insight into the direction towards a more ideal and wellbeing-conscious dietary routine. By embracing the core fundamentals of an even eating regimen—variety, segment guidelines, and careful utilization—we can furnish our bodies with sustenance, lift our spirits, and start a way toward top wellbeing and imperativeness. Let us, as we progress in our examination, recognize the heap of tastes and impressions that the normal world gives and relish the joy of reveling in our inward prosperity.

Perception of Macronutrients

Inside the perplexing domain of sustenance, macronutrients act as the central impetuses, providing the body with the fundamental energy and underlying parts to prosper. This part gives a more thorough assessment of macronutrients, including their capabilities, starting points, and ideal utilization levels to advance general wellbeing and health.

Sugars, which are fundamental to an even eating routine and the body's favored energy source, are at the vanguard of our examination. We investigate the capability of sugars in supporting our everyday exercises, including providing energy to our psyches' mental capabilities and working with muscle constriction during exercise. A separation is made between basic starches, including refined sugars, and complex carbs, which are overwhelmingly present in entire cereals, organic products, and vegetables. This qualification highlights the meaning of choosing wellsprings of starches that are wealthy in supplements, as they work with supported energy and add to by and large prosperity.

Besides, our center moves to proteins, which are basic parts of life and are fundamental for safe capability, muscle development, and fix. We explore the extensive variety of protein sources that are available to us, including plant-based choices like vegetables, nuts, seeds, and tofu, as well as creature-based choices like meat, poultry, fish, and dairy. The meaning of incorporating a different scope of protein sources into one's dietary routine is pondered to ensure adequate utilization of crucial amino acids and advance all-encompassing prosperity and energy.

Notwithstanding starches and proteins, we direct our consideration towards fats—fundamental parts of the eating regimen that are frequently underrated in spite of their basic job in supplement osmosis, chemical creation, and cell capability support. In this talk, we look at the different classifications of dietary lipids—immersed fats, unsaturated fats, and trans fats—and dissect their particular effects on cardiovascular wellbeing and cholesterol levels. It is important to focus on the choice of nutritious fats, including polyunsaturated and monounsaturated fats that are available in food sources like olive oil, nuts, seeds, and greasy salmon. Then again, the utilization of soaked and trans fats, which are common in handled and broiled food sources, ought to be confined.

Essentially, this portion serves as an aid for navigating the many-sided domain of macronutrients, empowering perusers to make informed choices in regards to their dietary practices and wholesome utilization. Through an extensive cognizance of the capabilities, beginnings, and optimal utilization amounts of sugars, proteins, and lipids, one can stimulate their bodies, support their psyches, and start a journey toward top physical and mental prosperity. As our examination advances, let us recognize the extensive variety of foods that supply us with the fundamental macronutrients for ideal wellbeing and relish the delight of taking care of ourselves.

Boosting the Capability of Micronutrients

Inside the perplexing organization of nourishment, micronutrients act as unheralded legends—little yet intense—with sweeping effects on human wellbeing and, in general, government assistance. This segment dives into the space of micronutrients, looking at their crucial capabilities in supporting a large number of physiological cycles and maintaining general prosperity.

Our examination spins around the interesting domain of nutrients and minerals. Nutrients and minerals are fundamental supplements that serve a huge number of capabilities inside the body, including advancing mental capability and cardiovascular wellbeing and supporting insusceptible capability and bone wellbeing. An investigation is led into the wide assortment of nutrients, which incorporates both fat-solvent and water-solvent assortments (e.g., nutrients A, D, E, and K). This article inspects the starting points, works, and suggested day-to-day consumption levels of these fundamental supplements, underscoring the meaning of obtaining them through a different and even eating routine.

Moreover, our center moves to minerals, which are micronutrients that are central to life and support compound action, cell flagging, muscle withdrawal, and neuronal capability. We analyze the meaning of minerals, including calcium, magnesium, potassium, and iron, in terms of overall wellbeing and health. In particular, we explore their commitments to oxygen transport, electrolyte equilibrium, and bone wellbeing. We give commonsense proposals for coordinating mineral-thick food sources into our dietary routine, including vegetables, nuts, verdant vegetables, and seeds, to ensure adequate utilization of these crucial supplements.

Notwithstanding nutrients and minerals, we direct our consideration towards phytonutrients—bioactive mixtures found in plants—which offer a broad cluster of wellbeing benefits, including, but not limited to, calming and safe help, cardiovascular wellbeing advancement, and persistent illness counteraction. An assessment is based on an extensive variety of phytonutrients, including carotenoids, flavonoids, and polyphenols, with an investigation of their starting points and expected benefits to wellbeing. We give sober-minded suggestions for coordinating phytonutrient-thick food sources into our dietary routine, including natural products, vegetables, spices, and flavors, to benefit from their restorative properties and upgrade general wellbeing.

This section can be a praise to the limit of micronutrients to give sustenance to the body, rouse inspiration, and work with the quest for the most extreme wellbeing and imperativeness. By procuring information in regards to the capabilities and starting points of phytonutrients, minerals, nutrients, and minerals, we can empower ourselves to pursue all-around informed choices in regards to our dietary practices and ensure the securement of fundamental supplements essential for ideal wellbeing. Allow us to additionally examine the heap of flavors and supplements that nature gives and recognize the significant effect that micronutrients can have on upgrading the strength of our physical, mental, and otherworldly creatures.

Viable Ideas for Feast Arranging and Shopping for Food

A sound eating regimen is laid out upon the synchronized rhythm of feast planning and the enthusiastic walkways of the supermarket. This segment investigates the realistic components of staple buying and feast arranging, giving proposals and strategies to help perusers explore the plenty of accessible food choices and gather nutritious meals, even dinners.

Fundamental to our examination is the capability of shopping for food—an ability that can empower us to choose more nutritious food varieties and further our wholesome targets. We give viable counsel to exploring the passageways of the general store, including how to peruse food marks and recognize supplement-rich food varieties, as well as how to make and stick to a buying list. New produce, lean proteins, and entire grains are regularly situated along the border of the store; thusly, it is critical to restrict the use of handled and bundled food sources that are high in undesirable fats, added sugars, and sodium.

Moreover, our center moves to feast arranging, which fills in as an urgent instrument in ensuring the accessibility of support and even dinners throughout the span of the week. Dinner arranging's benefits, which incorporate time and cost reserve funds, diminished food squander, and the advancement of better eating practices, are talked about. To work with dinner readiness, we provide functional feast arranging systems, including designating time every week for dinner arranging, fostering a week-by-week menu, and planning fixings in advance.

Notwithstanding dinner planning, we dig into the meaning of feast preparation and cluster cooking—aa period productive strategy that can help us keep up with our dietary targets in spite of chaotic timetables. We examine the upsides of group cooking, including the capacity to get ready and piece together huge amounts of fixings or dishes for sometime later. To work with dinner gathering, we give feast arrangement counsel, including strategies for cooking cereals, marinating proteins, and hacking vegetables ahead of time.

Essentially, this section serves as a realistic manual for perusers to engage themselves in dealing with the complexities of basic food item buying and dinner arranging, consequently empowering them to proactively oversee their dietary practices and advance their general wellbeing and health. By incorporating these down-to-earth suggestions and strategies into our everyday timetables, we can streamline our food choices, accomplish time and monetary investment funds, and assure the accessibility of supporting, even feasts that support our bodies and energy levels. As our examination endures, may we sincerely recognize the significant effect that feast arranging and readiness can have on cultivating a more strong and wellbeing-conscious lifestyle.

| 4 |

Chapter 4: Nutritional Needs for Older Adults

Understanding the Most Common Way of Maturing

As we progress through the course of history, our actual selves experience a remarkable succession of changes, every one of which lastingly affects our general wellbeing and condition. This part dives into a broad assessment of the maturing system, uncovering the mind-boggling interrelation between physiological changes and dietary prerequisites in individuals beyond 50 years old.

Our campaign requires a more significant understanding of the physiological changes that correspond with the maturing system. An investigation of the complexities of digestion is attempted, enveloping the intricate interchange of biochemical cycles that supply energy to the body and administer its expenses. With the movement old enough, there is a characteristic deceleration in the digestion, which brings about an ever-evolving decrease in energy requests and a raised vulnerability to weight gain and metabolic problems. Through the investigation of metabolic riddles, important information is procured in regards to the alteration of dietary examples to advance supported wellbeing and, generally speaking, prosperity in advanced age.

Moreover, we are faced with the awkward truth that absorption decline is an innate part of the maturing system and can impede the use and digestion of supplements from food. We look at the assorted scope of outcomes that can emerge from age-related changes in stomach-related capability, including adjusted gastrointestinal motility and diminished stomach corrosive discharge, which can affect nourishing status and overall wellbeing. By coordinating logical information with commonsense direction, we empower perusers to obtain information that illuminates their dietary choices and supplement utilization, ensuring that they satisfy the developing prerequisites of their bodies as they progress in age.

At the center of our talk is the affirmation that nourishment altogether impacts the avoidance of age-related medical problems and the advancement of solid maturation. In this review, we explore the meaning of fundamental supplements, including fiber, calcium, and vitamin D, in advancing stomach-related wellbeing, resistance capability, and bone wellbeing among the elderly. Attention to the unmistakable health prerequisites of individuals who are 50 or older empowers the customization of dietary interventions to neutralize the impacts of maturing and advance general prosperity and life.

This part essentially works as a foundation in our undertaking to fathom the complicated elements that exist among sustenance and maturing. Through the investigation of the conundrums encompassing the maturing system and its suggestions for dietary necessities, we empower perusers to expect organization over their wellbeing directions, each feeding choice in turn. As our examination endures, may we earnestly embrace the outlook-changing capability of information and establish the groundwork for a really encouraging and dynamic future during our brilliant years.

Fundamental Supplements for Maturing Wellbeing

Inside the complex texture of human nourishment, explicit supplements expect the job of essential support points that maintain the construction of wellbeing and imperativeness, especially during the later phases of life. This specific fragment investigates the mind-boggling domain of fundamental supplements that are basic for the most common way of maturing strongly, enlightening their crucial capabilities in encouraging general health and determination in people aged 50 or more.

One of the essential subjects of examination is calcium, a fundamental mineral that comprises the primary trustworthiness of the skeleton and is indispensable for the protection of bone wellbeing. The probability of creating osteoporosis and bone breaks increases with age, underscoring the criticality of keeping up with adequate calcium utilization to shield skeletal respectability and decline the likelihood of debilitating cracks. This article investigates an extensive variety of calcium-rich food varieties, including invigorated drinks, dairy items, and verdant vegetables, and gives down-to-earth guidance on the best way to integrate these supplement-rich food varieties into our regular routines.

Besides, our center moves to vitamin D, a fundamental supplement that is available in the sun and has broad consequences for safe capability, bone wellbeing, and general government assistance. With the movement old enough, the body's capacity to create vitamin D from daylight reduces, highlighting the criticality of consuming this fundamental supplement through supplementation or dietary means. We research the capability of vitamin D to work with calcium absorption, support the insusceptible framework, and relieve the probability of creating constant infirmities, including osteoporosis, cardiovascular illness, and explicit types of malignant growth. We give commonsense proposals for coordinating vitamin D-rich foods into our eating regimen, including greasy fish, eggs, and braced dairy items. Moreover, we underline the meaning of steady sunlight-based openness to maintain ideal degrees of vitamin D.

Notwithstanding calcium and vitamin D, we feature the meaning of fiber as a dietary hero because of its various medical advantages, which incorporate bringing down the risk of constant illnesses like coronary illness, diabetes, and explicit malignancies and advancing routineness and stomach-related wellbeing. The meaning of dietary fiber increases with age, as it supports the upkeep of solid entrails, the guideline of glucose, and the advancement of cardiovascular capability. This article looks at many food varieties that are bountiful in fiber, like natural products, vegetables, entire grains, nuts, seeds, and vegetables. It additionally gives a down-to-earth exhortation on the most proficient method to integrate these supplement-rich food sources into our day-to-day schedules.

Generally, this fragment has capabilities with respect to the fundamental supplements that comprise the bedrock of ideal maturation. By understanding the basic capabilities that calcium, vitamin D, and fiber play in advancing resistant capability, bone wellbeing, and general prosperity, we can equip ourselves with the information important to settle on taught choices in regards to our dietary examples and wholesome utilization. Give us access to our undertaking to perceive the significant effect that supplement-rich food varieties can have and establish the groundwork for a more hearty and empowering later life.

Levels of Suggested Everyday Admission

Especially as we cross the territory of maturing, it is important to understand the endorsed day-to-day admission levels of fundamental supplements within the perplexing embroidery of nourishment. This part inspects the exact suggestions in regards to the utilization of fiber, calcium, and vitamin D, with an accentuation on how these rules advance the general wellbeing and health of people who are 50 or older.

Vital to our examination is the recommended everyday utilization of calcium, which is crucial to keeping up with sound bones and skeletal trustworthiness. The day-to-day calcium admission proposals for people aged 50 or older show fluctuation, ranging from 1000 to 1200 milligrams overall. This article investigates the different determinants of calcium needs, including age, orientation, and hormonal status. It gives pragmatic counsel on the most proficient method to accomplish the suggested calcium consumption by consolidating sustained refreshments, supplements, dairy items, verdant greens, and invigorated drinks into one's eating routine.

Further, our center movements to vitamin D, which is ordinarily alluded to as the "daylight nutrient" and is fundamental for resistant capability, calcium retention, and by and large wellbeing. The day-to-day vitamin D admission rules for adults aged 50 or older are, for the most part, larger in size than those for more youthful adults, ranging from 600 to 800 global units (IU). In this talk, we address the different determinants that influence the need for vitamin D, including geological area, sun openness, skin pigmentation, and greasy fish utilization. Also, we give commonsense ideas for satisfying these proposals by means of dietary enhancements, eggs, invigorated dairy items, and greasy fish.

Notwithstanding calcium and vitamin D, we examine the ideal day-to-day utilization of fiber, a dietary component that has broad ramifications for cardiovascular wellbeing, stomach-related wellbeing, and general government assistance. As a rule, the recommended everyday fiber utilization for adults who are 50 or older is more noteworthy than that of more youthful adults, averaging somewhere in the range of 21 to 30 grams for ladies and 30 to 38 grams for men. We purposefully define complying with these rules by devouring a grouping of food sources bountiful in fiber, like organic products, vegetables, entire grains, nuts, seeds, and vegetables. We additionally provide logical ways to flawlessly coordinate these supplement-rich food sources into our regular dietary routine.

This segment has the capability to assist people beyond 50 years old in exploring the perplexing landscape of endorsed everyday admission levels for fundamental supplements. By having information on the suggested day-to-day recompenses for fiber, calcium, and vitamin D, we can empower ourselves to settle on very educated choices with respect to our dietary practices and the assurance that we fulfill the advancing wholesome prerequisites of our bodies as we age. Give us perseverance in accessing our undertaking to perceive the significant effect that supplemented food sources can have and establish the groundwork for a more strong and invigorating later life.

Dietary Variation for Changing Necessities

Our healthful necessities likewise go through changes as the dregs of time progress beneath us, requiring a nuanced way to deal with both eating regimen and way of life. This part digs into the meaning of repaying calories for the developing prerequisites of people aged 50 or more, giving practical ways to safeguard ideal wellbeing and prosperity all through the maturing system.

The groundwork of our examination is the affirmation that dietary prerequisites change as people age, inferable from impacts like metabolic and stomach-related framework adjustments as well as way of life decisions. The course of supplement absorption and use reduces with age, highlighting the criticality of consolidating supplement-rich food sources and dietary methodologies that advance ideal outcomes. The meaning of supplement thickness—the extent of imperative supplements to calories—in advancing general wellbeing and guaranteeing satisfactory nourishment in the elderly is analyzed.

Moreover, our center moves to approaches for enlarging caloric utilization to support the developing energy prerequisites of people who are 50 or older. Helped by a decrease in actual work and a slower digestion, more seasoned people might require a diminished caloric intake to support their weight and energy balance. This article digs into the meaning of integrating thick food sources into one's eating routine, including lean proteins, sound lipids, and complex sugars, to advance ideal wellbeing, energy levels, and bulk. Functional procedures for enlarging caloric utilization while keeping up with dietary benefit are given, including the consolidation of supplement thick tidbits and food stretched from and the expansion of sound lipids to dinners.

Notwithstanding calorie limitation, we underline the meaning of regularly evaluating and observing one's eating routine to ensure satisfactory sustenance. In this review, we explore the capabilities of medical services experts, including enlisted dietitians, who are entrusted with conveying individualized nourishment guidance and bearing to senior residents. Our distribution gives logical ways to deal with common snags to keeping a solid eating routine in advanced age, including monetary limits, dental complexities, and medicine contradictions. Thusly, we empower perusers to embrace a proactive position in their quest for dietary and nourishing streamlining.

This part works as a compass, giving guidance on the best way to change dietary examples to satisfy the developing necessities of people aged 50 or more. By getting information about the complexities of nourishing necessities during advanced age and executing ways to deal with advanced ideal wellbeing and prosperity, we can empower ourselves to progress in years in an elegant, energetic, and dynamic way, overflowing with the energy to welcome each new day. In our continuous interest, may we sincerely recognize the significant effect that legitimate sustenance can have on our wellbeing and essentialness as we enter our brilliant years.

Ideal Maturing Advancement Through Sustenance

Nourishment expects the job of a powerful director in the orchestra of presence, planning the amicable connection of the physical, mental, and otherworldly circles. This closing section investigates the huge effect of nourishment on working with sound maturing, giving significant viewpoints and ways to empower individuals matured 50 or more to embrace a dynamic and fulfilling presence.

Integral to our examination is the affirmation that nourishment fills in as something beyond a method for food; it goes about as an impetus for change, a major part of imperativeness, and a basic determinant of maturing-related wellbeing and prosperity. An investigation is directed at the broad repercussions of nourishment on more seasoned people, incorporating the advancement of actual wellbeing, mental capability, profound prosperity, and social association. Through the utilization of nutritious and healthy food sources, we can brace our invulnerable frameworks and forestall age-related medical problems like mental deterioration, cardiovascular sickness, and osteoporosis.

Besides, we shift our concentration towards the significant effect that nourishment can have on encouraging mental and profound health later on. We research the huge impact that dietary choices have on mental capability, mind-set, and cerebrum wellbeing, accentuating the criticality of consolidating cancer prevention agent-rich, omega-3 unsaturated fat, and other supplement-rich food varieties into one's eating routine. Mental capability can be saved, memory and focus can be improved, and a feeling of direction and satisfaction can be sustained during the brilliant years through the utilization of supplement-rich food varieties and support in friendly connections that invigorate the psyche.

Notwithstanding the domains of the physical and mental, we underline the meaning of nourishment in developing a more grounded sense of direction and association later on and sustaining the soul. An assessment leads to the significant effect that careful feasting can have. This training advances the development of appreciation for the sustenance that food offers, as well as a more grounded association with the current second through the relishing of its flavors, surfaces, and smells. By recognizing the significant effect that sustenance can have on one's wellbeing, imperativeness, and feeling of satisfaction during advanced age, we can start a course of maturing that is great, packed with joy, energy, and importance.

This part works as a tribute to the significant effect that sustenance has on advancing solid maturing and developing a dynamic, fulfilling presence among people aged 50 or more. Through the reception of careful eating standards, the utilization of supplement-rich food sources to support the body, and the development of a more significant consciousness of one's environmental elements and self, one can present to oneself the capacity to mature in an elegant, lively, and vivacious way, in this manner embracing each spending day. In our continuous interest, may we sincerely recognize the significant effect that legitimate nourishment can have on our wellbeing and essentialness as we enter our brilliant years.

| 5 |

Chapter 5: The Mediterranean Diet: A Blueprint for Healthy Aging

A Concise Outline of the Mediterranean Eating Routine

Inside the mind-boggling organization of wholesome methods of reasoning and dietary examples, just the Mediterranean eating routine has gotten similar logical approval and recognition. It isn't only a dietary routine; rather, a lifestyle is significantly imbued in culture, custom, and the plentiful produce of the Mediterranean Ocean's sun-doused lands. This section initiates an examination of the Mediterranean eating regimen as a model for advancing sound maturation. It digs into its broad, authentic foundation, central standards, and huge benefits for people during their later years.

The Mediterranean eating regimen is a well-established custom that has given sustenance to generations through its wealth of supporting, healthy food sources. It's anything but a passing oddity or pattern. The Mediterranean eating routine, which started in nations lining the Mediterranean Ocean (Greece, Italy, and Spain), is an embroidery of the culinary legacy of these districts, comprising the most delicious fish, sweet-smelling entire grains, freshest leafy foods, and fragrant olive oil.

On a very basic level, the Mediterranean eating routine is recognized by its bounty of plant-determined food varieties—an extravagant collection of the abundance presented naturally—including organic products, vegetables, nuts, and seeds. As well as providing sustenance, these food varieties likewise act as a wellspring of imperativeness by outfitting the body with fiber, cell reinforcements, and fundamental supplements that protect against disease and upgrade general wellbeing. Furthermore, the Mediterranean eating routine puts critical accentuation on heart-sound fats, lean proteins, entire grains, and red meat, while confining the utilization of handled food varieties, added sugars, and handled food varieties. This dietary routine lines up with the crucial standards of control, equilibrium, and agreement.

A top-to-bottom investigation of the Mediterranean eating routine uncovers an overflow of wellbeing benefits that rise above the area of dietary parts. A broad group of studies has reliably shown that it actually mitigates the probability of creating ongoing afflictions like cardiovascular illness, diabetes, malignant growth, and neurodegenerative issues. Besides, it advances life span and altogether works on personal satisfaction during advanced age. The key isn't exclusively in the constituent components of the eating regimen, but rather in the agreeable collaboration of its fluctuating variety of food varieties, supplements, and bioactive mixtures—aa gastronomic orchestra that gives food to the physical, mental, and profound creatures.

The Mediterranean eating regimen rises above its dietary part and addresses a lifestyle—aa demonstration of the significant relationship that exists between culture, wellbeing, and cooking. As we initiate our examination concerning the Mediterranean eating regimen as for solid maturing, may we sincerely embrace the people of yore's direction, relish the flavors local to the district, and start a journey toward a more hearty and wellbeing-conscious future during our brilliant years.

Looking at the Positive Pieces of the Mediterranean Eating Schedule

By totally embracing the Mediterranean eating standard, one tracks down an abundance of prosperity that transcends the area of central food. This part endeavors an assessment concerning the significant prosperity and flourishing implications of the Mediterranean eating standard, focusing in on its striking skill to provide food, ailment confirmation, and life expectancy progression, especially for individuals pushing toward old age.

The foundation of the Mediterranean eating routine is an abundance of supplement-rich, whole food sources that are clearly sourced from the ocean and land. Conveying an abundance of fundamental supplements, minerals, and cell fortifications, verdant food varieties are a certifiable jackpot of information that upholds the immune structure, balances disturbance, and shields against oxidative strain—the focal connection responsible for the start of steady illnesses and the developing framework. By embracing the dietary principles of the Mediterranean, which center around plant-based food assortments, we can update our supporting status and assure ideal prosperity all through our later years.

Moreover, the Mediterranean eating routine fills in as a paragon of cardiovascular prosperity, giving a flood of lean proteins and heart-sound lipids that help cardiovascular prosperity and lower the likelihood of stroke and coronary disease. Olive oil, a chief piece of Mediterranean gastronomy, is rich in monounsaturated fats and strong cell fortifications, including oleic destructive and polyphenols. These unsaturated fats and cell fortifications help in the reduction of irritation, cholesterol levels, and cardiovascular disease. Further, by decreasing heartbeat, greasy oil levels, and the likelihood of arrhythmias and blood thickening, oily fish use, which is abundant in omega-3 unsaturated fats, propels cardiovascular prosperity.

The Mediterranean eating routine has been associated with a decreased risk of steady illnesses, including diabetes, threatening development, and neurodegenerative issues like Alzheimer's disease, despite its cardiovascular advantages. The thought of a wide variety of supplement-rich food sources in the Mediterranean eating routine, including nuts, seeds, whole grains, and vegetables, adds to mental capacity support, glucose change, and the progression of sound handling. These benefits at last achieve a decreased risk of age-related infections and work on private fulfillment during the later periods of life.

The Mediterranean eating routine envelops a comprehensive method for managing food that sees the connection between the body, cerebrum, and soul. In this manner, it is more than a straightforward manual for additional prosperity. Through the gathering of the statutes of the Mediterranean eating routine and the blend of its nutritious, taking care of food sources into our conventional timetables, we can equip the critical capacity of food as medicine, subsequently spreading out a foundation for an all the more impressive and prosperous cognizant future.

Understanding the Consistent Guidelines Supporting the Mediterranean Eating Schedule

As our assessment of the Mediterranean eating routine advances, we further explore the legitimate confirmation that approaches the foundation of its extraordinary prosperity benefits. This part explains the wide gathering of assessments that demonstrates the ampleness of the Mediterranean eating routine in extending the future, letting the likelihood free from consistent sicknesses, and growing general government help among individuals matured at least 50.

Epidemiological assessments are the fundamental steps in the sensible cycle; they are expansive solicitations that have at least a time or two settled a strong connection between the Mediterranean eating standard and a diminished likelihood of making consistent diseases like cardiovascular disorder, diabetes, threatening development, and neurodegenerative issues. These examinations present persuading proof that the Mediterranean eating routine isn't just a social quirk yet rather an effective instrument for propelling prosperity and preventing disease, even as one ages.

Besides, clinical primers, which are seen as the best quality level for evaluating the impact of dietary mediations on prosperity results, have offered additional assistance for the Mediterranean eating schedule. The recently referenced fundamentals have given verification that the execution of a Mediterranean-style dietary routine can achieve enhancements in countless prosperity pointers, including provocative markers, circulatory strain, cholesterol levels, and glucose rules, which are huge in the beginning and movement of progressing illnesses.

The nuclear instruments by which the important effects of the Mediterranean eating routine on prosperity are applied have been edified by research. The Mediterranean eating routine includes an alternate assurance of plant-based food sources, including nuts, seeds, regular items, vegetables, whole grains, vegetables, and seeds. These food sources are abundant in bioactive combinations, which defend against oxidative tension, aggravation, and cell hurt through the synergistic action of phytochemicals, minerals, supplements, and minerals.

Besides, the positive macronutrient profile of the Mediterranean eating routine — contained a decreased usage of dealt with food assortments and submerged fats and an extended use of fiber, omega-3 unsaturated fats, and monounsaturated fats — helps with the smoothing out of metabolic capacity, the help of cardiovascular prosperity, and the balance of progressing diseases. By merging heart-sound lipids like olive oil and oily fish into the eating routine and zeroing in on whole, irrelevantly dealt with food assortments, the eating routine emphasizes food rather than constraint and spotlights on better standards if all else fails.

By and large, the Mediterranean eating routine is approved by an expansive and captivating assortment of consistent evidence, which gives significant solid areas for working with how we might interpret its critical prosperity benefits. Through the gathering of the statutes of the Mediterranean eating routine and the compromise of its enhancement rich food sources into our standard timetables, we can effectively utilize the huge effect of sustenance to vitalize life length, centrality, and complete government help during our splendid years.

Reasonable Ideas for Consolidating Dishes Motivated by the Mediterranean

As we initiate our undertaking to take on the Mediterranean eating routine as a model for ideal geriatric wellbeing, the requirement for common sense is of the utmost importance. This part gives the important instruments and techniques to really integrate Mediterranean-propelled feasts into our everyday schedules, ensuring a charming and persevering change to this nutritious dietary pattern.

The cycle begins with a psychological change—an affirmation that the Mediterranean eating regimen rises above being an assortment of dietary standards and, on second thought, addresses a way of life implanted with goodness, culture, and the appreciation for nutritious, tasty food sources. We take on an exploratory outlook and take on the Mediterranean eating routine with a responsive demeanor, as opposed to seeing it as a prohibitive routine, and on second thought, embrace the bunch of culinary open doors that it presents.

A principal attribute of the Mediterranean eating routine is its prioritization of occasional, new fixings—flavorful products of the soil, sweet-smelling flavors and spices, and premium proteins sourced from the sea and land. Advancing the utilization of negligibly handled, privately obtained food sources encourages an association with the world's abundance and the regular world's rhythms, in this way helping our wellbeing.

With respect to integrating another dietary routine, common sense is central, and the Mediterranean eating regimen is the same. We give sober-minded exhortations and ways to deal with consistently coordinating Mediterranean-roused dishes into our regular timetables, independent of monetary requirements, time limitations, or culinary capability. By giving shrewd recipe ideas and techniques for feast planning and group cooking, we empower perusers to find imaginative ways to integrate Mediterranean food into their day-to-day routines in a consistent and pleasurable way.

Besides, we dive into the idea of flavor matching, a gastronomic art that expands the gastronomic experience and the wholesome substance of feasts. Through the harmonization of variety, surface, and flavor, it is feasible to create tasty and satisfying dishes with a Mediterranean impact that enrapture the faculties as well as give them essentialness. The conceivable outcomes are, for all intents and purposes, boundless, going from appetizing olives and sweet, ready tomatoes to interesting citrus and velvety avocado.

The central part of taking on the Mediterranean eating routine involves more than simple dietary decisions; it likewise involves moving toward dinners with care, celebration, and a significant appreciation for the wholesome capability of each dish. By integrating practical counsel and strategies into our everyday routine, we can completely see the value in the gastronomic joys of the Mediterranean, mix our bodies with nutritious, entire food varieties bountiful in fundamental components, and start a journey toward a more vigorous and well-being-conscious later life.

Taking on the Mediterranean Lifestyle to Advance Wellbeing and Lifespan

As our examination concerning the Mediterranean eating regimen as a model for elevating solid maturing attracts to a nearby, we recognize that its benefits rise above the space of dietary parts. In this finishing-up portion, our consideration is coordinated towards the greater Mediterranean lifestyle—aa method of presence recognized by friendly cooperation, stimulating dinners, and a laid-back disposition. By completely embracing the Mediterranean way of life, people beyond 50 years old can bridle the total capability of this respected practice to improve their life span, essentialness, and generally prosperity.

Fundamental to the Mediterranean lifestyle is an appreciation for actual work—aa comprehension that movement is a lifestyle and not only a strategy for working out. The Mediterranean lifestyle advances actual work, versatility, and commitment to euphoric and indispensable pursuits consistently. This is exemplified through walking around the oceanside promenade, playing bocce ball with companions, or performing yoga in the nursery in the first part of the day. Participating in reliable actual work can add to the protection of bulk and strength, the advancement of cardiovascular wellbeing, and the upgrade of one's general condition of prosperity.

Besides, the Mediterranean lifestyle focuses on friendly cooperation, perceiving the crucial role that relational connections play in keeping up with one's physical, mental, and close-to-home prosperity. Taking part in social celebrations and festivities, imparting a dinner to loved ones, or joining a local area planting club are movements of every kind that add to the Mediterranean lifestyle. These exercises encourage a feeling of local area, backing, and fellowship, which improves our lives as well as reinforces our flexibility when faced with difficulty. Through developing social associations and sustaining significant connections, we can foster a feeling of direction, having a place, and satisfaction that gets through the difficulties and troubles of presence.

Past supporting actual work and social collaboration, disciples of the Mediterranean lifestyle embrace a laid-back position during feasts, perceiving that food fills in for pleasure, association, and delight as opposed to simple food. The Mediterranean way of life advances at an all the more relaxed pace during dinners, viewing them not just as physiological food but rather as events to see the value in the flavors, scents, and surfaces of one's food, devouring it carefully and thankfully while in the company of friends and family and partaking in the joys of the table. We can develop a sound connection with food, reduce pressure, and further develop processing, retention, and the general insight of our feasts by taking on a casual way to deal with eating.

The Mediterranean lifestyle encapsulates an exhaustive point of view on wellbeing and health, perceiving the relationship between the physical, mental, and profound parts of being. Through the fuse of reliable actual work, the development of huge social connections, and the reception of a laid-back dinner plan, people aged 50 or more can outfit the significant capability of the Mediterranean eating regimen to improve their life span, imperativeness, and general condition of wellbeing. As we progress along our way, may we sincerely take on the shrewdness of the Mediterranean lifestyle and lay out a way towards a more hearty and wellbeing-conscious later life.

| 6 |

Chapter 6: Cooking for One or Two

Acquiring Understanding of the Impediments Experienced in the Kitchen for Additional Minimized Families

In the midst of the peaceful beat of regular presence, the errand of giving food to oneself or a more modest family through the vehicle of cookery presents an unmistakable exhibit of hindrances. This segment enlightens the intricacies of the difficulties experienced by people who are relegated to the obligation of planning feasts for a couple or more. This work digs into the mind-boggling harmony that exists between imagination in the kitchen and reasonableness. Moreover, it recognizes the meaning of putting together feasts proficiently, directing bits, and diminishing food squander, especially within the imperatives of more modest families.

The campaign begins with a genuine acknowledgment of the potential difficulties that might emerge while planning feasts for a diminished group. Limited-scope feast arranging and part control are among the various intricacies that people experience while navigating the culinary climate of their families. These elements altogether differ from those that bigger families should fight with. Notwithstanding the undertaking of making sustaining and satisfying dinners, the test is to achieve this in a manner that is successful, practical, and strong for a balanced lifestyle.

Segment control is one of the essential obstructions that more modest families experience with regards to getting ready. In a general public where serving sizes and recipes are much of the time changed in accordance with obliged bigger get-togethers, people who are feeding a couple must capably deal with the test of adjusting adequate fixings to satisfy their craving needs without producing an excess of remains. An extensive knowledge of piece sizes and a preparation to change recipes and culinary methods to satisfy the prerequisites of a more modest family are fundamental for this undertaking.

Moreover, those responsible for planning feasts for more modest families could experience hardships concerning basic food item buying and dinner arrangements. As opposed to bigger families, which might find it more viable to plan feasts ahead of time and buy in amounts, people who are liable for feeding a couple should focus on the association of nutritious and changed dinners while keeping away from the compulsion to overload their fridge or storage space. This try requires fastidious planning, intelligent consultation on the flexibility of fixings, and a willingness to embrace simple and flexible dinner readiness.

Moreover, while taking special care of more modest families, people are faced with the squeezing matter of food squander, which turns into a significantly more noteworthy concern. Since transitory fixings are defenseless to decay preceding their total use, people genuinely must execute ways to deal with diminish squander and improve asset use. This might involve clever reusing of surplus fixings, fastidious fixing stockpiling and association, and a commitment to honest utilization and supportability.

Perceiving the principal impediments related to cooking for more modest families comprises an underlying step in overcoming those snags. By perceiving the particular elements and complexities that are characteristic of this gastronomic pursuit, people can plan strategies and goals that enable them to navigate the culinary territory with confirmation, resourcefulness, and adequacy. As our examination endures, may we earnestly jump all over the opportunity to reconceptualize getting ready feasts for a couple as an endeavor of gastronomic disclosure and self-food, overflowing with potential and confirmation.

Methods for Planning Feasts Productively

Productive menu arranging is a key part of culinary pursuits, especially for people getting ready for feasts for more modest families. This section uncovers an assortment of strategies intended to upgrade the course of feast arranging; they are strengthening and satisfying, as well as plausible and harmless to the ecosystem, to ensure that dinners. An investigation of the discipline of culinary association—aa fastidiously arranged ensemble of scents, flavors, and surfaces—is what this experience involves.

The underpinning of powerful feast arranging is established upon the guideline of foreknowledge—aa proactive position towards culinary planning that awards people the capacity to foresee their dietary prerequisites and inclinations in advance. Through the execution of a week-by-week feast plan, people can dodge the urgent quest for dinner motivation and fixings past the point of no return, subsequently working with a more smoothed-out and organized culinary experience. Dinner arranging furthermore gives the opportunity to work out some kind of harmony between flavor, assortment, and nourishment, in this manner ensuring feasts that are both nutritious and pleasurable.

A critical way to deal with powerful dinner arranging is the execution of cluster cookery, which is a period-proficient strategy including the pre-readiness and parceling of significant measures of nourishment for ensuing feasts. By distributing an assigned timeframe consistently for mass cooking, people can gather prepared-to-eat dinners in their fridge or cooler, reducing the need for everyday preparation and squandering food. Moreover, bunch cookery manages the cost of upgraded adaptability and creativity in the planning of feasts, as the remaining parts can be reutilized or coordinated into ensuing dinners.

An extra basic component of viable dinner arranging is the utilization of fixing flexibility, a culinary fundamental that promotes the determination of fixings that have the capacity to be used in various recipes and dishes. Through the intentional determination of versatile fixings, including grains, beans, vegetables, and proteins, one can easily set up a different cluster of dinners, deterring the need for broad storeroom loading or buying. This training smooths out the course of feast arranging as well as encourages creativity and reasonableness in the culinary area.

Moreover, viable dinner arranging requires intentional consideration of serving sizes and leftover food. By adjusting recipes to create decreased amounts or coordinating remaining parts into resulting feasts, people can really preserve culinary assets and alleviate food squander. A status to take on effortlessness and versatility during the time spent getting ready for dinners, alongside a devotion to reliable utilization and supportability, is vital for this.

In a general sense, compelling feast arranging fills in as proof of the significant effect that planning and design can have in the space of gastronomy. By carrying out strategies, for example, mass cooking, using flexible fixings, and practicing careful piece control, people who get ready dinners for more modest families can improve the productivity of their feast-arranging strategy, take advantage of their culinary assets, and start an undertaking into self-food and culinary advancement. With additional examination, may we embrace the act of viable feast arranging as a way to upgrade our culinary satisfaction, actual prosperity, and generally speaking, wellbeing.

Obtaining Capability in Clump Cooking

In the space of gastronomic skill, mass cooking emerges as a critical and sober-minded goal for people exploring the culinary territory of unassuming-scale families. This part investigates the act of mass cooking, a laid-out technique that empowers people to pre-get-ready dinners, decreases how much time is committed to the kitchen, and enhances effectiveness and comfort. This experience digs into the space of vital culinary preparation and planning—an amicable ensemble of tastes, surfaces, and scents carefully organized with reason and aim.

The crucial fundamental of group cooking is productivity, which involves purposeful work to upgrade culinary assets while diminishing waste by means of key readiness and arrangement. By dispensing an assigned timeframe consistently for mass cooking, people can collect various prepared-to-eat feasts in their cooler, in this way blocking the need for day-to-day cooking and reducing the tendency to rely upon comfort food varieties. Also, clump cooking gives the opportunity to exploit economies of scale by empowering the acquisition of fixings in enormous amounts, which can then be applied to various dishes.

A significant benefit of clump planning is that it energizes culinary development and assortment. The demonstration of preparing significant amounts of food empowers people to participate in culinary investigation and get more noteworthy joy from exploring different avenues regarding different recipes, flavors, and fixings. Moreover, group cooking advances the reception of dinner prep—aa system that involves pre-collecting parts and fixings—subsequently working with the get-together of feasts on tumultuous days or during occupied weeknights.

An extra basic component of mass cooking relates to its ability to reduce food waste. By protecting distributed feasts for individual holders and forestalling gorging, people can diminish the probability that extras will be squandered. Furthermore, group cooking improves segment control adaptability by allowing the customization of dishes to line up with explicit dietary necessities and individual inclinations. Thusly, one energizes reliable utilization and maintainability as well as ensures that feasts are delicious, flavorful, and new.

In a general sense, accomplishing skill in clump cookery fills in as proof of the significant effect that readiness and expectation can have inside the space of gastronomy. By taking on this customary strategy, people who get ready feasts for more modest families can improve the productivity of their dinner arrangements, amplify the utilization of their culinary assets, and start an investigation of culinary creativity and independence. Chasing further examination, may we sincerely take on the strategy of cluster cookery as a way to improve culinary satisfaction, efficiency, and generally government assistance?

The decrease in food squander

Inside the complicated domain of culinary pursuits, the persevering worry of food squander projects a threatening pall over the constant undertakings of people who plan dinners for more modest families. This segment resolves the common issue by analyzing approaches and solutions to diminish food waste and enhance culinary assets. This experience involves an investigation of upright utilization and maintainability—aa combination of creativity, genius, and significant appreciation for the world's abundant assets.

The groundwork of the work to decrease food squander is the care guideline, which involves a faithful way to deal with devouring and overseeing culinary assets. Through the execution of a careful way to deal with dinner arranging, staple buying, and cooking, people can limit the potential for squandered food and upgrade the usage of their fixings. This requires a status to plan feast arrangements involving the current fixings in the larder or fridge, rather than respecting the desire to unreasonably purchase or get ready.

A basic way to deal with food squander is through the execution of imaginative reusing, which is a culinary discipline described by the inventive change of unused fixings and leftovers into novel dishes. Through the use of creativity and cleverness in the culinary area, one can rejuvenate unused oats, proteins, vegetables, and different parts, changing them into tasteful and satisfying dishes. This training deters food squander as well as supports culinary advancement and investigation.

Moreover, the proper dealing with and course of action of short-lived products are essential elements in the decrease of food squander. The safeguarding of natural products, vegetables, and other transitory parts can be accomplished and kept up with in a drawn-out time span of usability using airtight holders or reusable packs. Besides, people can guarantee that nothing is squandered by monitoring their culinary assets by marking and dating holders containing extras.

A further vital component in the work to decrease food squander is the execution of careful utilization—aa conscious obligation to devour with aim and get joy from the scents, flavors, and surfaces of each and every feast. Through segment control, individuals can keep themselves from indulging and decline the probability that their remainders will be squandered. Besides, through intentional and continuous utilization, people can foster a more significant feeling of appreciation towards the food they ingest, consequently decreasing the tendency to waste.

At its center, the decrease in food squander fills in as proof of the significant effect that reliability and obligation can have in the area of gastronomy. People who get ready feasts for more modest families can improve the productivity of their culinary assets, limit wastage, and advance supportability through the execution of successful protection rehearses, imaginative reusing, and principled utilization. As we progress in our examination, may we embrace the thought of diminishing food squander as a way to improve culinary satisfaction, functional viability, and, in general, government assistance.

Nutritious and Clear Recipes for More Modest Segments

Inside the domain of gastronomic examination, the excellence of straightforwardness emerges as an overseeing standard for those planning dinners for more modest families. Inside this section, we present a combination of direct and feeding recipes modified solely for a couple of parts, introducing an amicable mix of fragrances, tastes, and surfaces that give food to the body and soul. It is an investigation of independence and culinary creativity—aa recognition of the joy and satisfaction gained from getting flavorful dinners ready with insignificant effort and maximal delight.

Vital to these recipes is an ethos of straightforwardness—an affirmation that planning supporting, flavorsome dishes isn't guaranteed to be difficult or time-consuming. These recipes incorporate a large number of feasts that are reasonable for more modest families, including good soups and mixed greens, one-pot dinners that are quick and simple to plan, and flexible grain bowls. Besides, every recipe is carefully intended to offer an amicable dietary profile, coordinating a collection of organic products, vegetables, entire cereals, and proteins to advance all-encompassing wellbeing and health.

A fundamental benefit of these recipes is their adaptability, which empowers cooks to customize their dishes as per their particular dietary and tangible necessities. Through fixing replacements, segment size changes, and personalization, these recipes give a road to culinary resourcefulness, empowering people to confer their own uniqueness to each dish. Additionally, a significant number of these recipes are purposefully created to be versatile and permissive, allowing a culinary act of spontaneity and investigation.

An extra vital component of these recipes is their prioritization of comfort and proficiency. Recognizing the restricted time and feverish timetables that people with more modest families make due, these recipes have been meticulously created to require just the absolute minimum of fixings and culinary time. These recipes take care of different dietary necessities, including make-ahead morning meals, speedy skillet dinners, chaotic weeknights, and relaxed ends of the week. They incorporate choices for slow cooker meals, sheet skillet dishes, and, surprisingly, sluggish ends of the week.

Besides, these recipes give priority to promptly possible and savvy fixings, accordingly guaranteeing that they are available to individuals from assorted culinary foundations and shifting monetary limits. Through an accentuation on simple, stimulating parts, including lean proteins, natural products, vegetables, and entire grains, these recipes represent that heavenly, nutritious feasts can be arranged reasonably and without the utilization of exceptional fixings. Alternately, they celebrate the abundance of the regular world's gifts and the joy they get from planning feasts with occasional, economical, and new fixings.

Generally, these clear and sustaining recipes stand as proof of the significant effect that resourcefulness in the kitchen and self-food can have on one's wellbeing. By taking on the core values of effectiveness, flexibility, and straightforwardness, people who get ready dinners for more modest families can get sufficiently close to a variety of tasty and satisfying dishes that give sustenance to the body and soul. As we progress in our examination, may we enjoy the scents, tastes, and surfaces of these recipes and begin a journey of gastronomic disclosure and independence that lifts our personal satisfaction and government assistance.

| 7 |

Chapter 7: Eating Out: Navigating Restaurants and Social Gatherings

Strategies for Choosing Better Choices While Eating Out

In the midst of the powerful texture of social commitment and gastronomic delights, eating out possesses an extraordinary position—aa second chance to participate in the satisfactions of both food and friendship. In any case, for the people who are endeavoring to maintain a balanced and nutritious dietary routine, the errand of exploring eatery menus might represent a huge number of snags. This part digs into the subject of pursuing wellbeing-conscious choices while feasting out, giving a broad scope of strategies and procedures to empower people to focus on their prosperity while still partaking in their dinner.

The groundwork of pursuing wellbeing-conscious choices while eating out is worth very much educated judgment. Outfitted with informed understanding and awareness, benefactors can move toward café menus with affirmation, perceiving the dietary piece of assorted courses and settling on options that are as per their wellbeing targets. In this examination, we analyze the meaning of menu scrutiny for explicit terms that show better techniques for arrangement, for example, "barbecued," "steamed," or "cooked." Alternately, we exhort staying away from dishes marked with terms like "seared," "breaded," or "smooth," as these terms habitually demonstrate raised amounts of impeding fats and calories.

Furthermore, segmenting the executives is essential for figuring out which food varieties to eat strongly while feasting out. To forestall overindulgence in a culture where tremendous segments have become the standard, people should rehearse care and poise. In this talk, we investigate techniques for segment control, incorporating offering courses to eating sidekicks or choosing canapé segments, notwithstanding procedures for seeing appetite and satiety signals to turn away the propensity to gorge.

An extra basic component of guaranteeing that feasting out is a stimulating encounter is knowing about the nourishing structure of the dishes served at cafés. People can explore the nourishing data of menu items ahead of time utilizing different apparatuses and assets, including eatery sites, versatile applications, and online data sets. By gaining data with respect to the dietary benefits of various dishes, including calories, fat, sodium, and sugar, people can engage themselves to settle on wise decisions that advance their general wellbeing and health.

Moreover, we investigate the idea of harmony and limitation, putting critical accentuation on the need to appreciate wanton food varieties with some restraint and, while practical, giving priority to choices that are plentiful in supplements. People can partake in the flavors and encounters of eatery dinners without feeling denied or remorseful by utilizing a reasonable way to deal with feasting out. We give proposals to enhance the healthy benefits of café feasts, incorporating beginning with stock-based soups or mixed greens, choosing lean sources of protein, and substituting vegetable-based sides or courses.

Generally, the groundwork for compelling food determination systems while feasting involves information, care, and awareness. By giving people the important assets and systems to capably and purposefully explore café menus, we empower them to enjoy the advantages of feasting out while remembering their physical and emotional wellbeing. Chasing further examination, may we sincerely embrace the act of choosing nutritious choices while eating out, as this will prompt expanded gustatory happiness, force, and life span.

Cognizance of Café Menus and Part Sizes

People who seek to maintain an even and nutritious eating regimen should have the principal capacities of exploring menus and fathoming segment sizes as they partake in the ensemble of culinary enjoyments that happen inside the limits of cafés. This segment digs into the intricacies of feasting in eateries, giving people the data and procedures important to pursue very educated choices that advance their physical and emotional well-being.

The endeavor begins with a top-to-bottom investigation of café menus—aa space described by a stupefying grouping of dishes, flavors, and gastronomic traditions. We embrace an assessment of the complexities present in menu portrayals, unraveling the etymological decisions utilized to portray various dishes, and separating between possibly unfortunate other options. By securing the capacity to perceive explicit catchphrases and expressions that show better techniques for planning, for example, "barbecued," "prepared," or "steamed," supporters can actually explore café menus and pick decisions that are as per their wellbeing goals.

Besides, segment control information is urgent for pursuing nutritious choices while eating out. To forestall overabundance in a culture where larger than usual segments have become the standard, people should rehearse care and poise. We investigate the idea of part control from top to bottom, giving methods for recognizing reasonable serving sizes and fighting the temptation to consume unnecessary amounts. Through the reception of control and the capacity to recognize yearning and satiety signals, people can participate in café feasts without encountering hardship or imperiling their wellbeing goals.

Moreover, we examine the concept of menu design, which foundations utilize as a procedure to influence clients' choices and reinforce income. Normal menu plan methods that are pondered incorporate the usage of text dimension, key situations, and estimating to underline explicit dishes and advance upselling. People can improve their menu route insight by obtaining information on the techniques used by cafés. This information will empower them to stay away from hasty purchasing and, on second thought, select choices that are as per their wellbeing goals and dietary inclinations.

Likewise, we look at the matter concerning the supply of surplus calories, sodium, and inconvenient lipids inside the foundation charge. Although some menu items might appear to be nutritious from the outset, they might contain secret fixings that compromise wellbeing targets. We give guidance on the most proficient method to recognize these hidden beginnings, including smooth sauces, dressings, and trimmings, and change or substitute them to set up a feast that is more nutritious. People can encounter delicious feasts that advance their wellbeing and prosperity by procuring the information important to stay away from the possible entanglements of eating in eateries.

On a very basic level, the capacity to translate café menus and understand segment sizes is basic for people endeavoring to maintain a balanced and nutritious dietary routine. By enriching themselves with data and philosophies to work with prudent choices, people can adroitly navigate the gastronomic territory of feasting foundations, savoring delicious charge while putting their physical and psychological well-being first. Allow us to additionally research the act of feasting out as a satisfying and supporting experience that helps the physical and profound creatures.

Ideas for Saving Social Associations While Putting Wellbeing as Fundamentally Important

In the midst of the jolly climate of parties and common feasts, it is absolutely critical to keep up with associations with loved ones. Be that as it may, people still up in the air to focus on their wellbeing might experience unmistakable challenges with regards to dealing with the social elements of feasting out. Inside this section, we embrace an investigation of the complicated balance that exists between developing social connections and maintaining individual wellbeing goals. We give logical direction and strategies to adroitly move through these conditions with balance and confidence.

Recognizing the meaning of compelling correspondence and emphaticness in friendly settings is the underlying step on the journey. It is enthusiastically suggested that people declare their wellbeing prerequisites and inclinations with affirmation and regard by proactively educating leaders and eating partners regarding their dietary limitations, inclinations, and goals. Advancing open and straightforward exchanges with respect to dietary prerequisites empowers people to encounter a feeling of consideration and backing in friendly conditions, while at the same time shielding their wellbeing goals.

Moreover, we look at the thought of adaptability and versatility in friendly settings, recognizing that not all eating experiences will be as one with a singular's wellbeing targets. Rather than viewing inconsistent extravagances as occurrences of falling flat, it is suggested that people embrace a nuanced and adjusted technique with regards to social devouring. This approach would allow adaptability and joy while maintaining a commitment to one's general wellbeing and prosperity. By cultivating a demeanor of adaptability and versatility, individuals and people in general can be more quiet and guaranteed during get-togethers, permitting them to see the value in the organization of others while maintaining a wellbeing-conscious methodology.

Besides, we give useful suggestions for finding more nutritious decisions in friendly conditions, including checking menus for lighter passage, choosing dishes that contain lean sources of protein, and while doable, consolidating vegetables and entire grains. In our conversation, we investigate different ways to deal with improving the health benefits of feasts by subbing or changing menu items. These incorporate suggesting that toppings and sauces be served independently, choosing arrangements that are barbecued or steamed, and deciding in favor of more modest piece sizes. By furnishing people with the fundamental data and assets to settle on informed choices in regards to their wellbeing in friendly conditions, we ensure that they can see the value in the organization of others without undermining their wellbeing targets.

Also, we examine non-regular eating choices in cafés that give opportunities for social collaboration while keeping up with wellbeing goals. There are countless strategies to love the organization of valued ones while keeping an emphasis on one's wellbeing, including planning culinary classes, open-air picnics, and potluck suppers. People can encourage their general prosperity through the improvement of lovely and essential social encounters through inventive and flighty reasoning.

In a general sense, finding some kind of harmony among wellbeing and social commitments requires successful correspondence, flexibility, and resourcefulness. By embracing these standards and strategies, people can move toward parties and culinary encounters with balance and class, getting joy from the organization of others while at the same time maintaining their wellbeing targets. Allow us to embrace the joy of social association and the profound and actual sustenance it gives as we proceed with our examination.

Acknowledgment of Careful Eating Techniques

In the steadily changing domain of social collaborations and devouring at cafés, the idea of careful eating emerges as a key rule that directs the people who want to maintain an amicable and nutritious association with food. Inside this specific section, we start an investigation into the domain of careful eating, digging into the significant effect that awareness, presence, and thought expectation can have on the culinary experience.

The basic principle of careful eating is the idea of presence—aa devotion to being totally charmed by the tactile experience of devouring food, enveloping the preferences and surfaces as well as the substantial impressions of craving and satiety. An investigation is embraced of the dietary act of decelerate eating, enjoying each significant piece, and fostering a significant appreciation for the food that food outfits. By integrating care into their eating experience, individuals can develop a greater appreciation for their food and obtain a greater comprehension of their dietary inclinations and prerequisites.

Moreover, careful eating is a strong instrument for partition control and the counteraction of overabundance. Through fostering an attention to appetite and satiety flags and taking part in deliberate eating, individuals can improve their capacity to control their food utilization and dodge the charm of devouring past their bodies' expectations. Strategies for recognizing actual cravings from close to home or ecological boosts are investigated, along with ways to deal with developing balance and self-empathy when faced with extravagances and hungers.

Besides, an assessment of the capability of care to advance a more sure self-perception and food relationship is embraced. Through the act of care in regards to the contemplations and feelings that arise all through the demonstration of consumption, individuals can possibly encourage an upgraded identity, sympathy, and acknowledgment, absent any and all regret or judgment. Approaches for recognizing and defying inconvenient mental examples related to food and self-perception are pondered. These strategies incorporate taking on an outlook of non-judgment towards oneself as well as other people and developing appreciation for the food that food manages.

Furthermore, we examine the connection between the patient's care and stomach-related wellbeing, underscoring the expected advantages of careful dietary practices on supplement assimilation and absorption. Through the act of careful and intentional eating, people can work with the stomach-related interaction and osmosis of fundamental supplements, consequently moderating the probability of stomach-related uneasiness and cultivating comprehensive wellbeing. Useful ideas for integrating care into the feasting experience are given, including the following: stop between nibbles to evaluate craving and completion prompts; bite food gradually and totally; and take a couple of full breaths before eating.

Advancing careful eating practices can be viewed as an intense instrument for people who wish to foster a more adjusted and wellbeing-conscious association with food. Through purposeful aim, mindfulness, and awareness during the eating experience, individuals can mix their bodies and spirits with improved understanding and sympathy. As we progress in our examination, may we sincerely embrace the significant effect that care has on the eating experience and relish the delight and food it brings to our reality.

Expecting and setting oneself up

In the midst of free-for-all of social commitment and eating journeys, people who are devoted to maintaining a sound and adjusted lifestyle perceive the outrageous significance of deliberation and readiness. This finishing-up portion dives into the space of expectation and preparation, giving commonsense direction and strategies to empower people to explore eating-out experiences easily and with affirmation.

The undertaking begins with an affirmation of the criticality of status in laying out the establishment for accomplishment. By taking part in proactive preparation and exhibiting premonition in regards to likely hindrances, people can move toward their encounters, feasting out with readiness and courage. We explore ways to deal with directing pre-dinner research on eatery menus, utilizing web assets, portable applications, and client assessments to observe nutritious other options and show up at all around informed choices. Besides, we are purposeful in the meaning of proactively advising the eatery work force regarding dietary limitations and inclinations. This guarantees that supporters experience a feeling of help and convenience all through their culinary undertakings.

Moreover, being arranged envelops realistic elements, including segment control and dinner timing, notwithstanding menu research. Our association helps with coordinating dinners and rewards, fully expecting get-togethers and eating out, accordingly guaranteeing that benefactors show up at feasting foundations feeling content and all around fed instead of exorbitantly eager or enticed to indulge. Besides, techniques to control segment sizes and fight the temptation to overabundance are thought after, including the act of imparting dinners to feasting buddies and the solicitation for more modest servings when they become something that anyone could hope to find.

Also, we dive into the idea of proactive dynamic inside friendly settings, which empowers individuals to apply organization to their feasting encounters and select choices that are as per their wellbeing targets. We are conscious of ways to deal with the prevailing difficulty and its companion impact with self-control and confirmation.

For example, we investigate thoughtful refusals of food or liquor offers that go against a person's dietary inclinations or targets. Through the foundation of unambiguous cutoff points and the prioritization of individual cleanliness in shared settings, individuals can all the while relish the organization of others and maintain their physical and emotional wellness.

Besides, we purposefully consider the meaning of adaptability and versatility with regards to eating out, recognizing that few out of every odd feast will unfold as planned. By fostering a mentality described by courage and openness, individuals can adroitly move through unanticipated hindrances or changes in procedures, keeping up with their commitment to prosperity while at the same time valuing the eccentrics and enjoyment of social connections.

Readiness and proactive planning are key capabilities that people should have to maintain a solid and balanced lifestyle when faced with social commitments and feasting. Through the reception of proactive measures, readiness, and adaptability, people can capably cross the gastronomic territory, savoring the satisfactions of eating out while at the same time setting their physical and emotional well-being first. In summary, let us finish up our examination by recognizing that prescience and readiness are imperative resources for chasing a prosperous, solid, and satisfying presence.

| 8 |

Chapter 8: Managing Special Dietary Needs

A Fathom of Continuous Dietary Limits and Sensitivities

It is essential to have a thorough understanding of normal limitations and sensitivities within the complicated domain of dietary prerequisites, especially as individuals age and experience physiological changes that might deteriorate previous circumstances or present novel obstructions. This segment dives into the domain of dietary limitations and sensitivities, explaining the physiological changes that might actually add to the expanded predominance of these circumstances in advanced age. We completely look at the intricacies of dietary difficulties like gluten narrow-mindedness, lactose bigotry, food sensitivities, and awareness. We give important insights into the side effects, triggers, and executive procedures related to these circumstances.

The interaction begins with an improved cognizance of the physiological changes that unfold with propelling age, which might affect a person's ability to get through specific substances and food sources. This study explores the impact of hormonal vaccinations, safe reactions, and stomach-related capabilities on conditions including gluten awareness, lactose tolerance, and food sensitivities. Thusly, it helps people recognize the signs and appearances of these circumstances, empowering them to look for reasonable direction and backing.

Besides, we completely analyze the intricacies related to predominant dietary limitations and sensitivities, giving clarity and understanding in regards to their starting points and side effects. By diving into the complexities of these circumstances—going from the immune system response prompted by gluten in those with celiac sickness to the deficiency of a chemical that results in lactose bigotry—we empower people to obtain the information important to pursue very educated choices in regards to their dietary and way of life decisions. Through acquiring knowledge of the crucial instruments that administer these circumstances, people can improve their capacity to control side effects and embrace proactive measures that advance their general wellbeing and government assistance.

Besides, we examine the implications of dietary limitations and sensitivities on comprehensive prosperity and ways of life, considering the physiological, mental, and cultural results of these issues. We give systems for beating the hindrances that people might experience while sticking to prohibitive eating regimens, including nervousness, disappointment, and sensations of confinement, to keep an uplifting outlook. By perceiving the extensive consequences of dietary limitations and sensitivities, we can improve our capacity to help individuals deal with these deterrents with backbone, manners, and compassion.

Likewise, we take part in a talk with respect to the meaning of customized sustenance and tweaked procedures for the administration of dietary restrictions and responsive qualities. In spite of the fact that there are generalizable dietary rules, it is important to recognize that each individual is particular and that what is successful for one individual may not really be powerful for another. This review investigates the capability of customized nourishment guidance, hereditary testing, and disposal regimens to help people perceive their triggers and form new ways to productively deal with their dietary prerequisites.

Essentially, acquiring information about common dietary limitations and responsive qualities is a basic part of helping individuals in their quest for the most extreme wellbeing and health. Through explaining the complexities of these circumstances and giving viewpoints on their etiology, side effects, and ways to deal with the executives, we present organizations to people, empowering them to consider reasonably their dietary and way of life choices. This engages them to defy the hindrances related to dietary limitations and sensitivities with confirmation, mettle, and levelheadedness.

Feast Plans and Recipes Adjusted to Exceptional Eating Regimens

In the midst of the broad domain of culinary investigation, people with extraordinary dietary prerequisites are directed by the standard of variation. With the rising noticeable quality of dietary limitations and sensitivities, it becomes basic to adjust feast plans and recipes to satisfy these prerequisites. This segment digs into the space of culinary inventiveness by giving guidance on the most proficient method to change recipes, and the feast intends to stick to the limitations of specific weight control plans. Thusly, we ensure that people can enjoy heavenly and satisfying feasts that advance their general wellbeing and health.

The endeavor starts with an inside-out assessment of the discipline of recipe change—an examination of the innumerable techniques by which customary recipes can be changed to satisfy the prerequisites of individuals who have food sensitivities or dietary limitations. We explore fixing replacements, including the utilization of sans dairy choices to milk and cheddar, gluten flours instead of wheat flour, and egg replacers for people with egg sensitivities. Through the reception of imaginative reasoning and versatility in culinary expressions, people can rethink their favored dishes in a way that sticks to their dietary limitations while still keeping up with the substance of flavor and happiness.

Also, we investigate the idea of dinner-making arrangements for people with extraordinary dietary requirements and give sober-minded exhortations and ways to deal with creating nutritious and even feast designs that record specific dietary limitations and sensitivities. An assessment of the meaning of equilibrium and assortment in dinner arranging follows, with an accentuation on coordinating a wide range of organic products, vegetables, entire cereals, and proteins to ensure adequate supplement utilization while evading common allergens and aggravations. People can improve their capacity to satisfy their dietary necessities and enjoy nutritious dinners by taking on a proactive role in feast arranging.

Likewise, we examine the meaning of culinary development and trial and error with regards to adjusting recipes and feasts to suit the requirements of people on unique eating regimens because of their culinary imagination. We furnish people with inspiration and motivation to explore novel fixings, flavors, and culinary techniques, embracing the opportunity to uncover heavenly and satisfying substitutes for their favorite cooking. By embracing a disposition of request and a responsive mentality towards recipe change, people can find plenty of culinary open doors and get delight and satisfaction from the demonstration of planning and eating food.

Furthermore, we intend for sober-minded elements to be considered while changing feast plans and recipes to suit social conditions and eating out. We give direction on successfully passing dietary necessities and inclinations on to masters and eating associates, notwithstanding strategies for exploring eatery menus and choosing dishes that are as per one's sensitivities and dietary limitations. By furnishing people with the vital data and assets to change recipes and feast plans for different conditions, we empower them to participate in satisfactory and nutritious dinners that advance their general wellbeing and health, regardless of their dietary limitations.

Dinner arranging and recipe variation for extraordinary weight control plans is, at its center, an undertaking requiring creativity, examination, and trial and error. By embracing culinary advancement and imagination in the kitchen, people can appreciate satisfactory and satisfying dinners that advance their wellbeing and prosperity, as well as exhibit regard for their dietary limitations and sensitivities. Allow us to additionally think about the significant effect that development and flexibility have on the space of gastronomic investigation and relish the joy and satisfaction we get from planning and consuming heavenly and nutritious dinners modified to suit our particular necessities.

Feasting Out and Exploring Social Conditions with Exceptional Eating Regimens

In the midst of the mind-boggling exchange of social commitment and mutual repasts, overseeing extraordinary dietary prerequisites while feasting out requires adroitness, successful correspondence, and a component of creativity. This part digs into the space of social feasting, giving realistic proposals and strategies to people with specific dietary requirements to easily explore get-togethers, guaranteeing that they might enjoy the organization of others while maintaining their dietary impediments and sensitivities.

Recognizing the meaning of viable correspondence and decisiveness in friendly settings is the underlying step in the journey. It is strongly suggested that people state their dietary prerequisites and inclinations with confirmation and regard, participating in open discussions with masters and eating associates in regards to their sensitivity-related concerns and dietary limitations. Advancing genuine and straightforward discourse with respect to dietary necessities empowers people to encounter a feeling of consideration and backing in friendly conditions, while at the same time defending their wellbeing goals.

Moreover, we explore commonsense ways to deal with actually overseeing unique dietary necessities while feasting out and in friendly conditions. We give proposals for directing pre-supper menu examination by using portable applications and online assets to recognize fitting choices and show up at very educated choices. To guarantee that dishes stick to one's dietary prerequisites, we additionally deliberate on strategies for imparting dietary necessities and inclinations to café staff, including asking about conceivable fixing replacements and readiness procedures.

Perceiving that few out of every odd feast will happen as planned, we become more conscious of the meaning of adaptability and versatility in friendly eating encounters. We help with really overseeing unexpected deterrents or changes in accordance with one's timetable by keeping a positive outlook and focusing on the delight gained from social commitment rather than becoming distracted by dietary limitations or impediments. By drawing in adaptability and versatility, people can easily and unhesitatingly explore get-togethers, permitting them to see the value in the organization of others while at the same time maintaining their wellbeing goals.

Moreover, we explore the meaning of development and imagination in the quest for options in contrast to ordinary culinary encounters. Working with social bonds with valued ones while at the same time taking care of dietary limitations can be accomplished in a countless number of ways, including putting together culinary classes, potluck suppers, and outside picnics. By embracing imaginative and unpredictable ways to deal with customary feasting-out encounters, people have the chance to participate in important and pleasurable social communications that add to their general wellbeing and health.

On a very basic level, overseeing exceptional dietary necessities while exploring social circumstances and eating out requires the use of correspondence, adaptability, and creativity. By incorporating standards of straightforward correspondence, flexibility, and development into common feasting experiences, visitors can see the value in the organization of others while at the same time considering their dietary restrictions and sensitivities. Let us, as we progress in our examination, remember the monstrous worth of social collaboration and the physical and otherworldly food it confers, while perceiving and esteeming our own wellbeing prerequisites.

Finding encouraging groups of people and assets for extraordinary eating regimens

At the point when people are faced with the difficulties of crossing the intricacies of dietary limitations and sensitivities, finding assets and encouraging groups of people can be of incredible help, furnishing them with empowering words, data, and courses. This part dives into the domain of encouraging groups of people and assets, giving people specific weight control plans with a comprehension of the plenty of assets available to them, and empowering them to effectively seek after the help they expect to prosper.

Recognizing the meaning of local area and association in the administration of extraordinary dietary necessities is the underlying step in the excursion. People with specific dietary requirements can find consolation, functional arrangements, and approval by means of online discussions, support gatherings, and local area associations. These assets empower those to explore their dietary limitations with certainty and grit. By forming associations with similar people who have experienced practically identical obstructions and hardships, people can gain important information, trade methodologies and strategies, and find backing and friendship in their quest for top wellbeing and health.

Moreover, we examine the capability of medical care professionals to offer individualized care and help to patients who have explicit dietary prerequisites. Medical care experts, including allergists, gastroenterologists, enrolled dietitians, and nutritionists, are of fundamental significance in helping people perceive their triggers, control their side effects, and form individualized ways to deal with their dietary requirements. People can upgrade their capacity to oversee dietary limitations and sensitivities with certainty and determination by talking with affirmed specialists here. Such experts can offer custom-made direction and help.

Besides, we are purposeful on the meaning of staying learned and momentum with respect to the latest headways and exploration in the space of specific eating regimens. An overflow of respectable sites and distributions, logical examinations, clinical preliminaries, and different sources furnish people with the resources to instruct themselves on their dietary requirements and explore novel treatment options, or the board draws near. People can advocate for their wellbeing prerequisites and pursue very educated decisions in regards to their eating regimens and ways of life by staying educated and enabled.

Likewise, we explore the capability of activism and promotion by focusing on the challenges and necessities of individuals with specific eating regimens. There are multitudinous ways in which people can encourage a more comprehensive and strong climate for people with dietary limitations and sensitivities, including upholding regulation, commanding menu naming, and advancing better openness and inclusivity in food choices. By standing up and supporting positive change, people can contribute to the production of a world in which all people, regardless of their dietary necessities, can participate in flavorful and nutritious dinners that advance their wellbeing and prosperity.

Finding encouraging groups of people and assets for people with exceptional dietary requirements is, at its core, a course of promotion, strengthening, and association. Through laying out associations with similar people, looking for the guidance and backing of qualified experts, staying all around educated and engaged, and upholding for helpful change, people can really explore the intricacies related to overseeing unique dietary necessities while keeping a cool head, strength, and poise. Allow us to recognize the limits of local areas and associations and help people in their quest for ideal wellbeing and prosperity as we progress in our examination.

Advancing Inclusivity and Variety in Food Determinations

Variety and inclusivity arise as core values for people with exceptional dietary prerequisites within the richly embroidered artwork of culinary investigation. During this finishing-up portion, we investigate the huge field of culinary variety, regarding the multitudinous surfaces, tastes, and customs that are plentiful in the space of gastronomy. We additionally give people inspiration and motivation to embrace a widely inclusive and varied dietary way of thinking, independent of their dietary limits and sensitivities.

Beginning the campaign is a remembrance of the distinguished social heritage and gastronomic traditions that have impacted the domain of food. There is a wealth of culinary variety to find and appreciate, going from the lively flavors of Indian cooking to the consoling kinds of Italian pasta dishes, and from the strong kinds of Mexican road food to the inconspicuous subtleties of Japanese sushi. Through the reception of a differing sense of taste, people can widen their culinary viewpoints, reveal beforehand unseen top choices, and get delight and satisfaction from the examination of unmistakable culinary customs and cooking styles.

Besides, we dig into the idea of inclusivity as to food determinations, recognizing the meaning of making arrangements for many dietary necessities and inclinations while eating in friendly conditions and at cafés. Guaranteeing that all supporters feel appreciated and a piece of the eating experience, giving straightforward fixing and allergen names, and offering an assortment of plant-based and sans gluten dinner choices are a couple of the methodologies we exhort in making comprehensive feast choices that oblige various dietary limitations and sensitivities. People can cultivate a steady and comprehensive climate by taking on a comprehensive way to deal with their food determinations. This would empower all visitors to participate in flavorful and nutritious feasts that accommodate their particular dietary prerequisites and inclinations.

Besides, the meaning of imagination and advancement in examining elective fixings and culinary strategies that oblige particular dietary prerequisites is thought. There is a broad assortment of plant-based options in contrast to meat and dairy items, as well as gluten-free cereals and flours, which can be used to prepare tasty and satisfying feasts while additionally taking care of explicit dietary necessities and individual inclinations. Through the reception of creative and trying methodologies in the culinary area, people can disclose new and enrapturing strategies to appreciate their favored food sources while at the same time giving recognition to their dietary impediments and sensitivities.

Furthermore, we dig into the thought of careful eating and develop a more significant proclivity towards food and its gastronomic encounter potential. A more profound appreciation for the flavors, surfaces, and smells of food, as well as an uplifted familiarity with the body's craving and completion signals, can be created by people who integrate care and presence into their feasting rehearsals. No matter what their food sensitivities and dietary limitations, people can determine more prominent happiness and fulfillment from their feasts by appreciating each chomp and eating with goal.

Essentially, embracing inclusivity and variety in culinary decisions involves an endeavor of examination, disclosure, and celebration. By embracing the immense range of culinary variety, creating feast choices that are comprehensive, researching elective fixings and cooking techniques, and taking part in careful eating, people can enjoy luscious and satisfying dinners that advance their wellbeing and prosperity, as well as regard their dietary limitations and sensitivities. As we draw nearer to our examination, may we remember the satisfaction and feeding substance that follow from embracing inclusivity and variety in our gastronomic choices and relish the abundance of the gastronomic domain that lies ahead.

| 9 |

Chapter 9: Maintaining a Healthy Weight and Body Composition

Appreciating the Troubles Engaged with Weight The board

Weight on the board is a fundamental part of complete prosperity in the field of wellbeing and health. In any case, as people progress in age, the difficulties related to exploring this territory escalate. This part digs into the perplexing deterrents that are natural for executives in advanced age, considering the many-sided collaboration of physiological, mental, and ecological components that can affect an individual's ability to achieve and support a solid body weight.

An inside-out assessment of the physiological changes that happen with age, which can significantly affect an individual's digestion, body organization, and weight guideline instruments, is the underlying step of the journey. As a singular age, their basal metabolic rate, bulk, chemical levels, and craving guidelines all abatement, which confounds matters extensively and can add to the expanded trouble of weight gain in advanced age. Through procuring information on the physiological components of activity, people can obtain a more profound comprehension of the unmistakable deterrents they could experience and form tweaked ways to successfully tackle them.

Moreover, we explore the mental and emotional determinants that might affect long-term weight on the board, including, but not limited to, mind-set problems, stress, adjustments in self-perception, and confidence. A huge number of life changes and stressors, including retirement, providing care commitments, and changes in friendly obligations, regularly go with the maturing system. These elements can affect a person's active work levels, dietary patterns, and general condition of wellbeing. Through a comprehension of the mental and close-to-home components of weight management, individuals have the chance to foster expanded mindfulness and strength, which will empower them to defy deterrents with self-control and resolve.

Moreover, we investigate the natural determinants that might affect long-term weight loss, including financial status, accessibility of nutritious dietary decisions, and cultural assumptions and standards. Especially for inhabitants of minimized networks, food uncertainty, confined accessibility of new produce, and the commonness of food deserts can be impressive deterrents to maintaining a sound weight and diet. By recognizing and handling foundational variations while upholding strategies that work with access to nutritious food varieties and guarantee food security, we can encourage a more helpful climate for seniors who wish to achieve and support a solid body weight.

Furthermore, the impacts of constant ailments and drug use on weight gain at an advanced age are analyzed. People with conditions like diabetes, hypertension, and joint pain might experience more prominent trouble dealing with their weight because of the effect of these circumstances on digestion, cravings, and active work. In like manner, explicit drug substances—including antidepressants, corticosteroids, and antipsychotics—may actuate weight gain or prompt modifications in hunger and digestion, subsequently adding to the intricacy of the circumstance. By teaming up intimately with medical care suppliers to regulate drug regimens and ongoing circumstances, people can at the same time seek out the weight the board targets while enhancing their wellbeing and prosperity.

Generally, acquiring a perception of the challenges related to weight gain during advanced age is an essential step towards empowering individuals to expect authority over their wellbeing and prosperity. Through a comprehension of the physiological, mental, and ecological determinants that affect executives, people can plan altered approaches that productively tackle these deterrents and effectively accomplish their wellbeing goals. Over our examination, may we take on an extensive perspective on the executives that perceive the complexities of the human condition and empower individuals to prosper all through their whole lives?

Techniques Upheld by Proof for Achieving and Supporting a Sound Body Weight

In the broad domain of weight, the executives value proof-based techniques and capabilities as core values, giving people logical instruments and procedures grounded in clinical proof and logical examination. This segment investigates proof-based systems that can help people in their later years achieve and sustain a solid weight. Thusly, they are enabled to make very educated choices in regards to their eating regimen, way of life, and schedules, which thusly work with the achievement of their weight targets.

The undertaking begins with an assessment of dietary strategies planned to work with the executives, accentuating the crucial precepts of piece guidelines and adjusted nourishment. It is basic to eat a variety of supplement-rich food sources from all nutrition types while likewise practicing segment control and energy utilization as a primary concern. Counts of calories plentiful in organic products, vegetables, entire oats, and lean proteins might work with weight reduction and upkeep, diminish desires, and advance satiety, as per the accessible proof. Through the implementation of a changed and balanced dietary routine that focuses on natural, entire food varieties, people can lay out a strong basis for long-term weight control and ideal wellbeing.

Moreover, we investigate the meaning of actual work in advancing weight for executives and general wellbeing. Standard actual work has been displayed to work with weight reduction through expanded calorie use, upgraded metabolic wellbeing, and upkeep of fit bulk, as indicated by a huge number of reviews. The weights the board targets are upheld by integrating actual work into day-to-day existence and finding pleasurable and reasonable types of activity, like yoga, strolling, swimming, cycling, or swimming. Through predictable commitment to active work, people have the ability to work on their general wellbeing and prosperity, in this way working with their undertakings to deal with their weight.

Moreover, an assessment is based on social techniques pointed toward overseeing weight, including, but not limited to, careful eating, objective foundation, and self-checking. Care work during dinners can build a person's familiarity with craving and satiety signals, bringing about more noteworthy part control and a lower caloric admission, as indicated by research. Going for the gold deficiency of one to two pounds each week is an illustration of a sensible and feasible objective that can help individuals in leftovers be persuaded and focused on their drawn-out progress. Through the reception of valuable ways of life, ways of behaving, and propensities, individuals can lay out a helpful environment that advances weight on the board and all-encompassing wellbeing.

Moreover, the meaning of social help and responsibility on the board is analyzed. Support from family, companions, or a care group has been shown to improve results and increase adherence to get-healthy plans, as per studies. People can keep up with their weight the board tries by getting consolation, inspiration, and responsibility through the demonstration of uncovering their goals and headways to other people. Moreover, people can profit from the individualized direction and backing of medical care experts, including enlisted dietitians and weight reduction advisors, to achieve their targets in regards to weight loss.

Essentially, proof-based ways to deal with achieving and supporting a solid body weight furnish people with logical instruments and systems grounded in clinical examination and logical request. Through the reception of an even eating regimen, steady commitment to actual work, execution of conduct systems, and seeking after friendly help, more established people can acquire the organization to deal with their weight and generally speaking wellbeing. Allow us to additionally research the adequacy of proof-based procedures to accomplish our weighted executive goals and have ideal existences throughout all periods of presence.

Coordination of actual work into regular schedules

Active work is a fundamental part of the structure for wellbeing and prosperity, giving many benefits to individuals of every age. This part dives into the space of actual work, looking at its importance in advancing long-term wellbeing and weight for executives, as well as giving practical counsel and ways to deal with coordinating active work into one's day-to-day daily schedule.

The investigation of the various benefits of predictable actual work for the board starts the journey. Active work has been demonstrated to increment calorie consumption, advance metabolic wellbeing, and support bulk, which are all variables in weight reduction and upkeep. Moreover, improved mind-set, perception, and personal satisfaction have been related to active work, notwithstanding a diminished risk of constant infections like diabetes, coronary illness, and explicit diseases. By integrating standard active work into their day-to-day schedules, people can work on their general wellbeing and prosperity while supporting the weight the board targets.

Besides, we investigate even-minded ways to incorporate actual work into one's day-to-day daily schedule, recognizing that chaotic plans and clashing commitments oftentimes render it hard to apportion time for active work. We give direction on the best way to find charming and harmless exercises for the ecosystem, like moving, walking, swimming, cycling, using the steps as opposed to the lift, or stopping a more prominent separation from the store, to integrate actual work into routine undertakings. By conceiving imaginative methodologies to incorporate active work into their day-to-day schedules, individuals can encounter the upsides of activity without demanding significant investment or exertion responsibilities.

Besides, we deliberated on the meaning of distinguishing proactive tasks that compare to individual tendencies and capacities, recognizing the shortfall of a generally pertinent methodology for working out. Whether it be participating in a walk around nature, partaking in a games association, or signing up for a gathering workout regime, it is fundamental to distinguish between charming, feasible, and effectively open exercises. Participating in pursuits that evoke sensations of bliss and satisfaction improves the probability that people will keep up with their obligations to them reliably, accordingly bringing about improvements to their general wellbeing and government assistance.

What's more, we dive into the idea of accidental actual work and its capability to add to the weight of the board and, by and large, prosperity. Little eruptions of action that come to pass over the span of the day, for example, strolling to the bus station, planting, or cleaning the house, are alluded to as accidental actual work. Albeit these exercises might seem irrelevant, they can possibly create significant calorie use bit by bit, consequently helping with energy equilibrium and weight management. By capitalizing on each potential chance to participate in coincidental actual work over the course of the day, individuals can build their general action level and aid in the accomplishment of the weight the executives target.

In a general sense, integrating actual work into one's everyday schedule is an undertaking of request, edification, and self-strengthening. By recognizing the complex benefits of steady actual work, searching out lovely and practical exercises, and quickly taking advantage of chances for serendipitous actual work, people can work on their general wellbeing and prosperity while supporting the weight the executives target. As we progress in our examination, may we honor the significant effect that active work has on people, all things considered, cultivating prosperity on both the physical and profound levels.

Grasping the Meaning of Nourishment in the Administration of Body Weight

Sustenance is a fundamental part of advancing wellbeing and prosperity, as it essentially impacts weight on the board and generally imperativeness. This segment looks at the complicated connection between sustenance and weight, with a specific spotlight on the standards of adjusted nourishment and their capability to help people over the long haul achieve and sustain a sound body weight.

An assessment of the meaning of adjusted sustenance in working with weight the executives goals starts the journey. A balanced dietary routine supplies the body with the important supplements for ideal working while likewise uplifting sensations of completion and satisfaction. By coordinating a different determination of supplement thick food varieties across all nutrition classes, people can really support their weight the executives try while at the same time meeting their nourishing prerequisites. The meaning of piece control and careful eating is pondered, with an accentuation on the advantages of going to yearning and satiety signals and checking energy utilization to accomplish a condition of ideal balance.

Moreover, we investigate specific dietary methodologies that might help with the quest for weight management goals. These incorporate putting an accent on entire, insignificantly handled food sources while diminishing the admission of undesirable lipids, added sugars, and refined grains. Eats less abundant in organic products, vegetables, entire cereals, and incline proteins have been shown to help with weight reduction and upkeep, decrease desires, and advance satiety. By integrating these food varieties into their day-to-day diet, people can create a helpful environment that advances compelling weight gain while at the same time giving their bodies crucial supplements.

Besides, the meaning of satisfactory hydration in advancing weight for executives and in general wellbeing is expounded upon. Reliably drinking adequate water over the course of the day can help with hydration, hunger guidelines, and metabolic help. We suggest integrating hydrating food sources into feasts and bites, conveying a reusable water container, and setting suggestions to polish off water over the course of the day. Furthermore, we recommend conveying a reusable water bottle and conveying hydrating vegetables and organic products for snacks.

What's more, we dig into the thought of feast arranging and readiness as pragmatic instruments that guide chasing after weight the executives goals. Taking part in proactive dinner arranging and readiness can help people avoid reliance on cheap food choices, practice segment control, and make more wellbeing-conscious food decisions. We give feast-arranging exhortations and procedures, including the production of a week-by-week dinner plan, the readiness and freezing of feasts in mass for later utilization, and the consolidation of different surfaces and flavors to keep feasts charming and fulfilling.

On a very basic level, it is basic to grasp the meaning of nourishment in order for executives to empower individuals to pursue very educated choices with respect to their way of life and dietary propensities. People can encourage a helpful air for weight loss and general wellbeing by taking on the precepts of adjusted sustenance, which incorporate eating negligibly handled, entire food sources, keeping up with satisfactory hydration, and dealing with their feasts ahead of time. As we progress in our examination, may we honor the significant effect that sustenance has on people's profound and actual wellbeing, supporting them in their quest for ideal health.

Conquering Impediments and Supporting Inspiration

Inside the intricate domain of weight on the board, the capacity to conquer hindrances and support inspiration turns into a basic inclination for making supported progress. This finishing-up portion investigates pervasive hindrances that people might face while endeavoring to deal with their weight. It likewise gives strategies for conquering these challenges and keeping up with inspiration to achieve and support a sound load from now on.

An assessment of average impediments to weighting the board, including time limits, stress, close-to-home eating, and cultural assumptions, comprises the underlying section of the journey. These snags often obstruct people's efforts to get more fit and make it challenging to keep up with their targets. Through the most common way of recognizing imminent obstructions and figuring out proactive techniques to defeat them, people can effectively explore difficulties with mettle and resolve.

Moreover, the meaning of taking care of oneself and self-sympathy in supporting goals connected with weight on the board is thought. Focusing on exercises that feed the body, psyche, and soul is taking care of oneself. Such exercises incorporate overseeing strain, guaranteeing sufficient rest, and partaking in pursuits that give joy and fulfillment. By focusing on their physical and profound wellbeing, people can foster the strength and backbone necessary to conquer hindrances and keep up with their inspiration during the course of weightlifting.

Moreover, we examine the meaning of social help in supporting responsibility and inspiration. Support from family, companions, or a care group has been shown to upgrade results and increase adherence to health improvement plans, as indicated by research. People can keep up with their weight when the executives try to get support, inspiration, and responsibility through the demonstration of uncovering their targets and headways to other people. Besides, people can profit from the individualized direction and backing of medical care experts, including enlisted dietitians and weight reduction guides, to accomplish their targets with respect to weight.

Moreover, the meaning of laying out functional and achievable targets for long-term weight on the board is pondered. Individuals are encouraged to lay out goals relating to adjustments in their way of life and conduct, as opposed to focusing solely on mathematical qualities. These targets might incorporate increasing active work levels, refining dietary determinations, or developing careful eating practices. Inspiring and moving people towards their drawn-out progress are little, achievable targets that are joined by achievement festivities.

Conquering obstructions and supporting inspiration are crucial skills that are basic for achieving and supporting a solid body weight during the later phases of life. Through the distinguishing proof of likely hindrances, the execution of taking care of oneself and self-empathy rehearses, the sale of outer help, and the foundation of achievable goals, people can conquer challenges with courage and resolve, subsequently keeping up with their inspiration all through their undertaking to deal with their weight. In outline, we ought to remember the adequacy of self-empathy, versatility, and assurance in helping individuals in their quest for ideal wellbeing and health.

| 10 |

Chapter 10: Mindful Eating and Emotional Health

Examining the Connection Between Food and Feelings

The unpredictable and complex interchange of food and feelings is a crucial part of the human condition, particularly as people progress through their later years. Inside this fragment, we start an edifying examination concerning this significant relationship, looking at how our feelings shape our association with food and, alternately, how the food sources we ingest can affect our profound condition.

Starting the excursion is an acknowledgment of the multifaceted and different qualities that contain this relationship. Food has been complicatedly connected with our close-to-home encounters since the early stages, working as a conductor for comfort, celebration, and relational holding. This relationship goes through a change with the progression of time, impacted by social shows, social turns of events, and individual experiences, among others. An investigation is led into the habits in which full of feeling states, including weariness, strain, and depression, can apply an effect on eating designs, possibly bringing about weight gain and in general unexpected problems.

Moreover, we dig into the idea of "solace food" and its capability of lightening our mental pain. Solace food sources, like a bowl of warm soup on a cold day or a piece of chocolate after a long day of work, habitually possess an extraordinary spot in our spirits because of the consolation and relief they give during troublesome times. An examination is directed at the mental systems that underlie this peculiarity, with an emphasis on how explicit food varieties can inspire feelings of comfort and memory, as well as deal with the transient lightening of close-to-home misery.

Moreover, we investigate the idea of "close-to-home yearning" as opposed to "actual craving" and stress the meaning of separating the two. Profound craving habitually introduces itself as sudden desires for specific food varieties, joined by a squeezing feeling of need and an insufficiency to satisfy hunger exclusively by feeding food sources. Through the improvement of better ways of dealing with stress and the capacity to recognize profound cravings from actual yearning, people can secure a more profound comprehension of their eating patterns and foster more powerful techniques for controlling their feelings.

Additionally, we explore the potential effect that our dietary inclinations might have on our mental condition. Certain supplements, including serotonin-helping food varieties like bananas and oats and omega-3 unsaturated fats tracked down in greasy salmon and salad greens, have been shown to influence mental capability and mindset emphatically. In actuality, there is proof to recommend that devouring an eating regimen bountiful in handled food varieties, sugar, and unfortunate lipids might lift the probability of creating sorrow and tension. Through the reception of a nutritious and even eating regimen, people can encourage strength and upgrade their profound wellbeing as they defy the different difficulties that emerge all through their lives.

On a very basic level, the relationship among people's cooking and feelings is a complicated texture of human life, impacted by social legacy, standard practices, and individual encounters. Through the utilization of curiosity and sympathy towards this relationship, individuals can gain a more significant comprehension of their eating designs, manufacture more salubrious and profound guideline techniques, and encourage a more amicable and nutritious association with food. Allow us to recognize the significant crossing points among food and feelings as we progress in our examination; these convergences give our lives importance, significance, and interconnection.

Perceiving the Meaning of Cognizant Utilization

In the midst of the speedy ideas of contemporary society, the act of careful eating emerges as an image of quietness, giving individuals a way to foster a more significant relationship with their food and bodies. This part dives into an inside-out assessment of careful eating, inspecting its significant ramifications for profound prosperity and the development of an agreeable association with food.

On a very basic level, careful feasting relates to how we devour food, not simply the substance. It urges us to move toward the demonstration of eating with an uplifted feeling of mindfulness and presence, empowering us to completely see the value in each chomp and give recognition to the sustenance that food confers. Through developing a consciousness of our faculties and decelerating our speed, we can all the more significantly understand the surfaces, aromas, and kinds of our food, accordingly upgrading our appreciation and satisfaction with our eating attempts.

Moreover, careful feasting gives a strong solution for the feverish and requesting qualities of contemporary presence. In the midst of a climate soaked with redirections and rushed eating times, careful feasting urges people to quickly reconnect with themselves by stopping, breathing, and zeroing in on the present. We can decrease strain, nervousness, and close-to-home eating ways of behaving by integrating care into our eating rehearsals. Therefore, we can move toward our feasts with self-control, clarity, and reason.

What's more, rehearsing careful eating works with the improvement of an increased consciousness of our interior signs in regards to craving and satiety, as it urges us to tune into our body's yearning and completion signals. By noticing the guidance of our bodies and possibly eating food when we are really starving, rather than in light of propensity or feeling, we can cultivate a more positive association with food and advance our profound government assistance.

Eating carefully additionally gives a chance to foster more noteworthy mindfulness and self-sympathy. By developing self-empathy and consideration, we can acquire understanding of our dietary patterns and examples by coordinating our consideration towards our viewpoints, feelings, and sensations during the demonstration of eating. Appreciating our apparent "errors" or "disappointments" in our eating ways of behaving with generosity and empathy is something contrary to self-analysis; it advances the improvement of a demeanor of resistance and steadiness when stood up to with snags.

In a general sense, the execution of careful feasting conveys huge implications for both our mental state and our association with food. We can foster more noteworthy mindfulness and self-sympathy, sustain a more significant association with our bodies and food, and lessen pressure and profound eating ways of behaving by integrating care into our eating rehearsals. Allow us to additionally explore the extraordinary capability of careful food as a way to fortify our physical, mental, and otherworldly creatures with each eating experience.

Techniques for Application to Encourage the Act of Careful Eating

At the point when people mean to foster a more significant association with their bodies and food, commonsense strategies are essential assets chasing careful eating. This part looks at a variety of procedures and activities that are explicitly created to expand care and mindfulness with regards to feasting. Thusly, people are enabled to move toward their feasts with a feeling of presence, goal, and appreciation.

A careful breath is considered a fundamental practice in the domain of careful eating. By coordinating our concentration towards our breath preceding, during, and resulting to dinners, we can lay out a condition of quietness and fixation while establishing ourselves right now. The execution of clear breathing strategies, like careful breathing contemplation or profound stomach breathing, can help individuals foster uplifted mindfulness and care during feasts.

Besides, body examinations provide a strong instrument for laying out an association with our actual selves and adjusting to real sensations. Taking part in a pre-dinner body examination wherein people mindfully perceive any locales of strain or misery and develop an unpretentious familiarity with these sensations, from the crown to the soles, can be beneficial. Taking part in this training might work with the improvement of an elevated aversion to the hunger and completion signs of the body, as well as a more strong trust in the body's knowledge.

Besides, rehearsing careful eating can help individuals develop a more profound sense of appreciation for the tangible experience of devouring food. One way in which people can participate in careful eating is by zeroing in on the experience of consuming a solitary raisin or piece of natural product with every one of their faculties locked in. Through the act of seeing the surface, variety, smell, flavor, and sound of the food, people can turn out to be totally charmed in the ongoing second and encourage a more profound respect for the food it confers.

Besides, people can participate in careful feasting through their conscious deceleration and enthusiasm for each nibble of their dinner. Individuals can improve their feasting experience by devoting time to consider biting, relishing the different flavors and surfaces of every significant piece, and taking care of the impressions of appetite and completion that manifest instead of racing through dinners or performing multiple tasks while eating. A more noteworthy feeling of fulfillment and appreciation can be gotten from feasts when one eats carefully, subsequently diminishing the likelihood of indulging or profound eating.

In a general sense, down-to-earth techniques for encouraging careful eating furnish people with an essential aid for developing uplifted cognizance and mindfulness in their feasting rehearsals. Through the day-to-day reconciliation of careful eating, body checks, careful breathing, and enjoying, people can cultivate a more profound association with their food and bodies, consequently adding to their general prosperity. As our examination advances, may we sincerely embrace these commonsense instruments for strengthening our physical, mental, and profound creatures with each piece.

Inspecting Profound Eating Examples

The perplexing interaction among food and feelings habitually leads to close-to-home eating ways of behaving, which represent an impressive obstruction for those meaning to foster a more good association with food and support their profound government assistance. This part dives into different ways to deal with defying close-to-home eating ways of behaving in a careful and merciful way, fully intent on enabling people to develop more valuable survival strategies and advance their profound prosperity by means of careful eating.

The undertaking begins with an acknowledgment of the unpredictable connection between feelings and dietary examples. Habitually, testing or horrendous feelings—like uneasiness, pressure, dejection, or bitterness—are overseen by close-to-home eating. Especially when encountering profound pain, people might fall back on food for the purpose of getting passing comfort. By and by, this method of adapting habitually brings about repeating episodes of pigging out, culpability, and embarrassment, which effectively demolish profound torment and support a common example of negative dietary ways of behaving.

Moreover, an investigation is directed into the meaning of recognizing impetuses that initiate profound eating and forming elective instruments for battling with sentiments that don't include food. Through developing care in regards to the considerations, feelings, and conditions that evoke episodes of profound eating, individuals can procure a more profound comprehension of their eating designs and lay out additional useful procedures for managing their feelings. To diminish pressure and nervousness, this might involve the execution of unwinding procedures like moderate muscle unwinding, profound breathing, or contemplation. On the other hand, people might track down comfort and close-to-home prosperity through a commitment to pleasurable pursuits, like investing energy with friends and family, chasing after private interests, or walking around indigenous habitats.

Besides, we examine the meaning of self-empathy and non-judgment with regards to dealing with close-to-home eating ways of behaving. People are educated to take on an outlook with respect to self-acknowledgment, understanding, and consideration towards themselves rather than self-analysis in regards to apparent "disappointments" or "mix-ups" in their eating rehearsals. People can figure out how to pardon themselves for past offenses and foster more noteworthy versatility, notwithstanding deterrents and difficulties, by developing self-empathy. This will empower them to proceed with their journey toward better dietary patterns with more noteworthy clarity and resolve.

What's more, we are intentional about looking for help from family, associates, or emotional well-being experts while endeavoring to conquer close-to-home eating ways of behaving. People can foster better survival techniques and get consolation, approval, and bearing to support the route of troublesome feelings by trusting in reliable mates with respect to their battles and hindrances. Besides, by counseling psychological wellness specialists, including advocates and advisors, people can acquire individualized direction and backing to handle central close-to-home worries and develop more useful components for overseeing strain and other testing feelings.

In a general sense, by moving toward close-to-home eating ways of behaving with care and empathy, individuals can develop a more profound condition and foster a more certain association with food. Through the distinguishing proof of close-to-home eating triggers, the improvement of elective survival strategies, the development of self-empathy, and the seeking of social help, people have the ability to free themselves from profound eating examples and encourage an upgraded condition of quietness, harmony, and backbone in both their dietary practices and profound prosperity. As our examination perseveres, may we earnestly and openly take on these methodologies, mindful of the way that each ever-evolving step brings us closer to upgraded profound health and fulfillment.

Advancing Profound Wellbeing through the Act of Careful Eating

Inside the great plan of things, careful eating shows itself as a strong instrument for developing profound wellbeing and advancing a harmonious association with food. This closing section dives into the significant ways in which careful eating can reinforce the profound wellbeing and general feeling of prosperity of people, empowering them to foster a greater degree of compatibility with their food, bodies, and selves.

Essentially, careful feasting urges us to participate in our dinners with a demeanor of readiness, purposefulness, and appreciation. Through purposeful deceleration and a significant feeling of delight, one can totally charm their faculties and become completely consumed in the tangible experience of eating, consequently developing a more significant appreciation for the food that food grants. By participating in this training, we encourage an expanded feeling of appreciation and happiness in our eating experiences, consequently developing a helpful and strong association with food.

Besides, careful feasting gives a sanctuary of serenity and harmony in the midst of the clutter of presence. In the midst of a contemporary society where food is habitually eclipsed by uneasiness and pressure, careful eating urges people to release their faculties, reconnect with themselves, and take a transient delay. We can decrease nervousness, stress, and profound eating ways of behaving by developing care during feasts. By guiding our focus toward our viewpoints, feelings, and sensations, we can move toward our feasts with poise, clarity, and presence.

What's more, careful feasting advances the act of paying attention to the body's natural direction in regards to craving and satiety. We can develop a better relationship with food and work on our consciousness of our physiological necessities by tuning into the signs of yearning and satiety that our bodies send. By putting less dependence on outside prompts or close-to-home triggers to direct our dietary patterns and on second thought, depending on the intrinsic insight of our bodies to support us, we can develop a more significant sense of identity, regard, and trust in our bodies.

Furthermore, this training provides a way to foster increased degrees of mindfulness and self-sympathy. By developing self-empathy and thoughtfulness, we can acquire knowledge about our dietary patterns and examples by coordinating our consideration towards our viewpoints, feelings, and sensations during the demonstration of eating.

Appreciating our apparent "slip-ups" or "disappointments" in our eating ways of behaving with consideration and empathy is something contrary to self-analysis; it advances the improvement of a demeanor of resilience and determination when defied with impediments.

Essentially, the act of careful eating gives people an aid for fostering a more significant feeling of serenity, harmony, and fulfillment in their association with both food and themselves, consequently encouraging profound prosperity. People can develop a more noteworthy feeling of association, concordance, and bliss in their lives, as well as work on their close-to-home wellbeing and prosperity, by consolidating the standards of appreciation, care, and presence into their eating rehearsals. Allow us to praise the groundbreaking force of careful eating to sustain our bodies, psyches, and spirits and to cultivate an existence of more prominent wellbeing, joy, and satisfaction as we attract to a nearby on this examination.

| 11 |

Chapter 11: Staying Hydrated: The Importance of Water and Fluid Intake

Perceiving the Significance of Satisfactory Hydration

In the midst of the perplexing transaction of physiological cycles, hardly any substances are as essential as water. Sufficient hydration is key to one's wellbeing and prosperity, coordinating an orchestra of physiological cycles inside the body as a quiet director. Inside this section, we start an investigation into the significant significance of supporting adequate hydration levels, explicitly as individuals explore the difficulties of advanced age.

Generally, water capabilities are the quintessence of the organic entity, empowering the basic cycles that are basic for our presence and thriving. Water serves a broad and fundamental capability, including everything from working with assimilation and moving imperative supplements to cells to controlling internal heat levels and lubricating joints. By underscoring the basic meaning of satisfactory hydration, we empower people to recognize water not exclusively as a consumable but as a central part of their comprehensive prosperity and vivacity.

Moreover, we investigate the complicated systems through which hydration impacts different aspects of wellbeing and, generally speaking, health. Sufficient hydration is fundamental for ideal mental capability, cardiovascular wellbeing, absorption, and osmosis of supplements. Also, adequate hydration is fundamental for working with the end of poisons from the body, supporting kidney capability, and keeping up with sound epidermis. By grasping the broad implications of hydration, people can foster an appreciation for its significance that reaches beyond essentially satiating thirst and recognize it as a basic part of extensive wellbeing and prosperity.

In addition, we research the unmistakable hindrances and elements to be considered with respect to hydration while analyzing the most common way of maturing. Hydration status can be affected by a few elements: remembering modifications for prescription use, changes in thirst discernment, and movement with age. Thus, it turns out to be more basic to focus on liquid admission. By enlightening these age-related factors, we empower people to really oversee potential obstructions to hydration and embrace deterrent measures to keep up with adequate hydration as they progress in age.

Essentially, understanding the significance of sufficient hydration lays out the basis for individuals to give priority to their liquid utilization and augment their comprehensive wellbeing and government assistance. Through recognizing water's importance as a pivotal supplement that supports imperativeness and works with physiological cycles, individuals can foster a more significant comprehension of the significance of hydration in their regular routines. As we progress in our examination, let us honor the significant effect that sufficient hydration has on our prosperity and imperativeness, as well as its ability to provide food and sustenance.

Researching Components That Impact Hydration Status

As one dives into the mind-boggling domain of hydration, it becomes obvious that a large number of components have an effect on the hydration status of an individual, particularly with age. Inside this specific section, we initiate an intriguing examination concerning these factors, clarifying the complexities that shape hydration levels and stressing the criticality of grasping and relieving them.

A fundamental element to remember while endeavoring to determine hydration status is the maturing system. The limit of the body's ability to control liquid homeostasis is compromised with age, bringing about adjustments to the perception of thirst and kidney capability. Therefore, senior residents might show reduced aversion to indications of thirst and experience the ill effects of crumbling renal capability, which can bring about weakened pee fixation and water maintenance. By recognizing these physiological changes related to maturing, people can embrace safeguard measures to guarantee that they keep up with adequate hydration levels.

Moreover, we investigate the impact of medications on hydration status, considering that many of the time-endorsed drugs can possibly upset the body's liquid balance. Certain antidepressants, diuretics, and antihypertensives can possibly alter electrolyte equilibrium and increase urinary results; in the event that liquid admission isn't properly changed, these medications might cause parchedness. Through information on the potential effects of drugs on hydration, patients can team up intimately with their clinical experts to supervise their hydration levels and make fundamental adjustments to their liquid utilization to limit any adverse results.

Besides, we research the effect of natural factors, including temperature, stickiness, and levels of actual work, on a singular's hydration status. Raised temperatures, significant mugginess, and enthusiastic active work can possibly expand sweat-prompted liquid misfortunes, consequently presenting individuals to an elevated risk of parchedness if their liquid utilization neglects to counterbalance these misfortunes adequately. By practicing consciousness of natural conditions and adjusting liquid utilization appropriately, individuals can improve their general wellbeing and prosperity by maintaining a legitimate hydration balance.

Also, the impact of prior ailments on hydration status is considered, considering that particular circumstances might expand a person's helplessness to drying out or liquid overabundance. Liquid homeostasis in the body can be upset by conditions like diabetes, kidney illness, and cardiovascular breakdown; thus, cautious checking of liquid admission and results is expected to forestall confusion. Through close coordination with medical service suppliers and adherence to customized hydration suggestions, people can improve their capacity to direct their hydration status and reinforce their general prosperity.

Looking at the factors that impact the condition of hydration gives people important information with respect to the complexities involved with maintaining an optimal balance of liquids. Through acquiring information on the manners by which hydration can be influenced by age-related changes, drugs, natural elements, and basic medical issues, people can embrace a proactive position to keep up with adequate hydration and advance their general wellbeing and prosperity. As our examination continues, may we take on the bits of knowledge procured from appreciating the intricacies of hydration and utilize them to empower us to put hydration at the forefront of our wellbeing-advancing methodologies.

Exhortation on the Best Way to Guarantee Adequate Liquid Admission

While taking a stab at the most elevated level of wellbeing and health, focusing on legitimate liquid utilization as a key part of taking care of oneself is basic. This part gives a broad assortment of soberminded guidance and strategies to empower people to support satisfactory degrees of hydration on a regular basis. By incorporating these direct yet solid techniques into their day-to-day regimens, individuals can advance their general wellbeing and imperativeness while taking care of their hydration prerequisites.

Water utilization over the course of the day is one of the most clear and effective techniques for guaranteeing adequate liquid utilization. Carrying out clocks on water vessels or setting updates can help people keep up with their hydration goals and guarantee reliable water utilization. Moreover, keeping a reusable water compartment in a consistent presence can work as a stylish way to remain hydrated and work with the demonstration of tasting water whenever of the day, be it at the workplace, at home, or while voyaging.

Additionally, people can expand their liquid utilization by incorporating food varieties that advance hydration into their dinners and eating. Products of the soil that are wealthy in water, including melon, strawberries, and oranges, as well as cucumbers, celery, and tomatoes, can possibly make significant commitments to a singular's day-to-day liquid utilization. Moreover, these food varieties supply imperative supplements and cell reinforcements. By integrating these hydrating food varieties into their weight control plans and munchies, individuals can advance their general wellbeing and prosperity while meeting their hydration prerequisites.

Besides, people can further develop their hydration levels by picking hydrating drinks rather than sweet or charged choices, for example, coconut water, home-grown imbuements, and mixed water. These drinks work with liquid utilization as well as give valuable wellbeing benefits, including electrolytes and cancer prevention agents, which advance hydration and, generally speaking, prosperity. By setting hydrating drinks above less nutritious options, people can actually support ideal hydration levels and advance their overall wellbeing.

Moreover, people can survey their hydration status through their perception of the variety and recurrence of their pee. For the most part, pee that is clear or light yellow means adequate hydration; on the other hand, hazier pee might show drying out and require an expansion in liquid utilization. Through excessively paying attention to their body's signs and, in this manner, changing their liquid utilization, people can support hydration harmony and advance their all-encompassing wellbeing and prosperity.

Additionally, people can further develop their hydration levels by integrating hydrating exercises into their everyday schedules. These practices might incorporate starting every day with a glass of water, polishing off water before dinners, and soaking up water while taking part in open-air exercises. By focusing on hydration and integrating these practices into their day-to-day schedules, people can improve their general wellbeing and essentialness while supporting their hydration prerequisites.

Essentially, by giving an exhortation on the most proficient method to ensure adequate liquid utilization, people are furnished with down-to-earth ways to support their hydration necessities and augment their comprehensive wellbeing and government assistance. By integrating these clear yet effective methodologies into their everyday timetables, individuals can lay out legitimate hydration as a key part of their own cleanliness and empower themselves to thrive in all aspects of their presence. As we further explore these ideas, may we sincerely and transparently embrace them, for each drink adds to our advancement towards further developed wellbeing and imperativeness.

Following up on the Discovery of Drying Out Signs

Amidst the high-speed nature of regular presence, it is habitually inconspicuous that our bodies offer unobtrusive signs when they accept that our degrees of hydration are deficient. This part investigates the pointers and appearances of drying out, empowering perusers to recognize circumstances in which their liquid balance might be compromised and to answer quickly with proper measures. By staying ready and responsive to these pointers, individuals can safeguard their physical and emotional well-being, as well as guarantee that they have adequate hydration.

Thirst, an undeniable sign of parchedness, is a physiological response impelled by the body's fundamental prerequisite for water. In spite of the fact that thirst might have all the earmarks of being an irrelevant sensation, it fundamentally illuminates the body that it is in need of hydration. It is prudent for people to quickly drink water after detecting thirst to reestablish exhausted liquids and deflect extra drying out.

Likewise, changes in the recurrence and shade of pee can yield huge data with respect to hydration status. Pee that is light yellow or straightforward by and large implies adequate hydration, while pee that is more obscure in variety might actually demonstrate parchedness. Also, people ought to endeavor to accomplish ordinary pee over the course of the day with respect to their urinary recurrence. Drying out can be gathered from a decrease in urinary recurrence or volume, requiring a prompt expansion in liquid utilization.

Moreover, people should be aware of extra physiological signs that could harmonize with drying out, including, but not limited to, weakness, dark circles underneath the eyes, a dried mouth, and unsteadiness. These side effects might work as pointers that the body is dried out and require critical clinical consideration. By immediately distinguishing and answering these markers, people can turn away the headway of drying out and advance their comprehensive wellbeing and prosperity.

Besides, people who are older or have explicit ailments might have an expanded powerlessness to dry out and ought to steadily screen these pointers. Lack of hydration helplessness can be expanded by prescription use, age-related changes in thirst discernment, and prior medical issues; along these lines, proactive measures to keep up with sufficient liquid equilibrium are required. By practicing steady carefulness and going to proactive lengths, people can diminish these dangers and guarantee that their hydration prerequisites are focused on.

On a very basic level, the capacity to recognize signs of parchedness and expeditiously answer furnishes people with a fundamental system to safeguard their physical and mental government assistance. By staying watchful of their body's physiological markers and quickly tending to signs of drying out, individuals can turn away intricacies and maintain ideal degrees of hydration. As our examination continues, may we reliably and fearlessly acclimatize to this data, perceiving that our faithful undertakings to keep up with satisfactory hydration add to our comprehensive prosperity and imperativeness.

Embracing Hydration as a Key Wellbeing Point of Support

Upon cautious examination of the perplexing transaction of hydration inside the human body, it becomes obvious that water isn't just a consumable but instead a fundamental remedy of life. This closing segment underlines the basic meaning of keeping up with sufficient hydration as a crucial part of general wellbeing and health. Through recognizing water as a basic supplement that supports essentialness and works with physiological cycles, individuals can foster a more significant comprehension of the meaning of hydration in their regular routines.

Hydration, on a very basic level, is an imperative part of our being, impacting essentially all features of our wellbeing and otherworldly state. Satisfactory hydration advances cardiovascular wellbeing, helps with temperature guidelines, and works with supplement osmosis, among other expansive and significant advantages. It likewise upholds mental capability. By putting sufficient hydration as an essential standard of wellbeing, individuals can cultivate the improvement of their physical, mental, and otherworldly selves, in this way boosting their general imperativeness and condition.

Besides, by perceiving the meaning of hydration as a key part of individual cleanliness, individuals are empowered to proactively take care of their hydration prerequisites and boost their general prosperity. By fostering an uplifted consciousness of their body's thirst signals, choosing hydrating food varieties and drinks, and sticking to basic yet successful procedures, for example, keeping a predictable water consumption, people can cultivate a more significant association with their bodies and sustain themselves inside.

Moreover, hydration capabilities are a powerful instrument in sustaining balance and imperativeness inside the creature, working with the ideal activity of physiological frameworks, and advancing equilibrium and congruity inside. Through the upkeep of adequate hydration, people can sustain their protection from stress, reinforce their safe framework, and advance their general prosperity, accordingly working with outcomes in all aspects of life.

Besides, by recognizing the meaning of hydration as a crucial part of prosperity, individuals are urged to think about their liquid utilization with care and reason, seeing each beverage as an opportunity to renew and sustain their actual creatures. Through the act of getting a charge out of water for what it really is and perceiving its imperative capability in supporting life, individuals can foster a more significant feeling of appreciation and worship for the presented asset of hydration.

On a very basic level, by perceiving hydration as a principal foundation of wellbeing, individuals can upgrade their essentialness, versatility, and general condition. Through recognizing the critical role that water plays in supporting physical processes and advancing general prosperity, individuals can lay out hydration as an essential part of their routine of taking care of themselves and bridle the significant capability of ideal hydration. As we draw nearer to our examination, may we celebrate the uncommon bestowal of hydration and recognize its major importance in keeping up with our wellbeing and imperativeness; for each ounce of water we polish off carries us one bit closer to improved health and essentialness.

| 12 |

Chapter 12: Planning for the Future: Nutrition and Longevity

Perceiving the Meaning of Sustenance in Encouraging Expanded Life Expectancy

As we progress through the course of our lives, the significant effect that sustenance has on our physical and psychological well-being turns out to be continuously more obvious. This segment looks at the critical effect that nourishment has on broadening the future and further developing the general prosperity of more seasoned people. An investigation is embraced into the complicated interrelationships among dietary examples, wellbeing results, and life span, fully intent on clarifying the significant impact that nourishment has on the most common way of maturing.

Basic to the issue is the comprehension that our dietary choices altogether affect the course of our wellbeing and life span. Sticking to an even and supplement-rich eating routine has been shown to considerably diminish the probability of creating persistent illnesses, including diabetes, coronary illness, and explicit kinds of malignant growth. These circumstances rank among the essential drivers of grimness and mortality in the later phases of life. By putting a higher value on entire food sources that are bountiful in phytonutrients, nutrients, minerals, and cell reinforcements, people can fortify their bodies against the impacts of maturing and establish the groundwork for a solid and fulfilling future.

Besides, the relationship between a person's nourishment and life span rises above the anticipation of infections and includes more exhaustive elements of wellbeing and, in general, prosperity. As well as giving sustenance to the body, an eating regimen rich in organic products, vegetables, entire cereals, lean proteins, and healthy fats advances ideal mental wellbeing, close-to-home prosperity, and mental capability. By giving the essential supplements to the ideal physical process, we lay out the foundation for a day-to-day existence described by energy, versatility, and imperativeness.

Besides, the impact of sustenance on the advancement of life span rises above the singular level and has broad ramifications for society in general. As medical care frameworks battle with the rising weight of persistent sickness and populations get older, the meaning of preventive measures, including the reception of solid dietary practices, turns out to be continuously obvious. By giving people the capacity to pursue all-around informed dietary choices and embrace solid way of life rehearses, it is feasible to mitigate the effects of ongoing illnesses, decline medical service consumption, and work on the general way of life for the elderly.

Essentially, grasping the meaning of nourishment in cultivating life span furnishes people with a masterful course of action to sustain wellbeing and imperativeness across the whole life expectancy. Through recognizing the critical impact that dietary choices have on by and large wellbeing and taking on an even, supplement-rich routine, individuals can upgrade their possibilities of achieving a delayed, sound, and satisfying presence. As we progress in our examination, may we celebrate the significant effect that sustenance has on our drawn-out wellbeing and the unrest it empowers us to encounter.

An Economical Philosophy for Advancing Refreshing Eating

It is critical that we utilize a practical way to deal with good diet that upholds our drawn-out wellbeing goals to accomplish life span and prosperity. This part investigates ways to deal with fostering a dietary arrangement that advances general health, feeds the body, and keeps up with imperativeness as we age.

The standards of control and balance are essential to a supportable arrangement for consuming strongly. Rather than respecting the enticements of stylish eating plans or outrageous dietary regimens, we advance the reception of an adaptable and balanced nourishing way of thinking that underlines the utilization of entire food varieties, assortments, and control. By remembering a wide assortment of supplement-rich food sources for our feasts and treats, we can ensure that our bodies are provided with the essential cell reinforcements, nutrients, and minerals to ideally work.

Besides, the idea of supportability rises above simple healthy benefits and encompasses more exhaustive elements, including social setting and ecological repercussions. Supporting nearby ranchers and advancing biodiversity by choosing occasional, privately obtained products at whatever point conceivable lessens our carbon footprint as well as advantages the climate. Likewise, by embracing culinary customs and social legacy, one can develop a more significant association with food and the local area while additionally upgrading the eating experience.

Also, careful dietary practices are of fundamental significance in advancing both prosperity and manageability. By fostering a mentality of care and being available during dinners, people can completely see the value in the preferences, surfaces, and scents of their food, fostering a more significant feeling of appreciation for the food they give. We can uphold our general wellbeing and prosperity by developing appreciation for the overflow of food on our plates, going to yearning and satiety signals, and eating relaxed to encourage a more amicable relationship with food.

In addition, manageability consolidates the cycles of creation, planning, and utilization of the food sources we eat. By taking on reasonable food works, including, but not limited to, food squander decrease, support for regenerative horticulture, and promotion for food equity, people can orchestrate their dietary choices with their own qualities and make productive commitments to worldwide drives. By embracing an exhaustive point of view on maintainability that considers the interdependencies among wellbeing, food, and the climate, we can lay out a food framework that is both really sustaining and versatile.

Essentially, by embracing a supportable dietary way of thinking, we gain the capacity to give sustenance to our bodies, defend the climate, and advance the soundness of the present and people in the future. By integrating supportability, equilibrium, and care into our dietary choices, we can encourage a lifestyle that advances wellbeing, essentialness, and satisfaction. Allow us to additionally examine the capability of practical sustenance to advance actual prosperity, local area improvement, and long-haul natural supportability.

Developing a Long Period of Empowering Schedules

It is pivotal that, as we navigate the way of presence, we embrace a mindset of ceaseless turning of events and self-conservation, explicitly with respect to our dietary practices. This segment digs into the meaning of embracing a drawn-out attitude toward sustenance, encouraging people to foster perseverance through dietary practices that cultivate actual wellbeing, imperativeness, and by and large health.

The groundwork for embracing a deep-rooted obligation to great sustenance is the comprehension that wellbeing is an interaction, not a proper endpoint, that is impacted by the choices we make consistently concerning our way of life and dietary practices. We exhort against seeing good dieting as a transient pursuit or a simple, necessary evil; all things being equal, we advocate for a comprehensive way to deal with sustenance that puts emphasis on maintainability, balance, and delight. By embracing a way of thinking of ceaseless schooling and self-improvement, we can reliably upgrade our dietary practices to offer all the more successfully to our drawn-out wellbeing and health.

Besides, the method involved with growing enduringly nutritious practices is described by headway instead of perfection. We advocate for self-empathy and versatility instead of the quest for dietary flawlessness or the accommodation of sensations of regret or disgrace when we veer off from our nourishing goals. Recognizing the dynamic and always changing nature of smart dieting empowers us to move toward our dietary process with curiosity, responsiveness, and flexibility, generously and acceptingly exploring the high points and low points of life.

Moreover, developing a positive relationship with food and our bodies is a basic part of taking on a long period of nutritious practices. We advocate for people to foster a disposition of appreciation towards food, instead of seeing it as a danger or a reason for culpability and embarrassment, because of the sustenance it offers. By developing a natural and agreeable eating style that considers the body's craving and satiety signals while valuing the preferences, surfaces, and smells of food, one can improve their general wellbeing and prosperity.

Besides, the advancement of perseverance through sound ways of behaving is improved by the friendship and help of individual people. On our dietary journey, building a local community of people who share our devotion to wellbeing and health can offer priceless inspiration, motivation, and responsibility. Whether through virtual networks, support gatherings, culinary clubs, or care groups, laying out connections and fostering a feeling of kinship with people who share our qualities and goals can rouse and tie us to our drawn-out wellbeing targets.

Generally, embracing a steady routine of supporting practices all through one's presence furnishes people with a way to improve their wellbeing, essentialness, and by and large condition. Through the execution of a drawn-out sustenance standpoint, the improvement of self-empathy and versatility, the advancement of a positive self-perception and relationship with food, and the requesting of social help, it is feasible to set out on a dietary excursion that is both persevering and valuable to our wellbeing and bliss. As our request advances, may we earnestly recognize the significant effect that getting through sound ways of behaving can have on our prosperity and promise to give our lives to self-sustenance.

Effectively Exploring Snags and Difficulties

It is pivotal that, in our quest for long-lasting, sound ways of behaving, we perceive and overcome the various obstructions and difficulties that might emerge. This segment dives into the predominant difficulties that people might face while on a dietary journey and offers sober-minded approaches for nimbly conquering them.

The commonality of problematic data and dietary patterns in the media and mainstream society is perhaps the most typical hindrance people experience while endeavoring to keep up with sound propensities. In a domain immersed in health powerhouses, diet plans, and trends, it very well may be hard to recognize reality and fiction and to explore the multifaceted territory of sustenance guidance. We encourage people to search out proof-based data from trustworthy sources, like enlisted dietitians, nourishment researchers, and respectable wellbeing associations, to conquer this obstruction. By outfitting themselves with exact and reliable data, individuals can proactively decide the best dietary practices they stick to and, in this way, keep themselves from being hoodwinked by misleading data.

Also, the upkeep of nutritious practices might be blocked by outside factors, including monetary requirements, time limits, and social or familial impacts. Prevailing burdens, chaotic timetables, and monetary restrictions can all add to the trouble of focusing on a sound eating routine and sticking to dietary targets. To conquer these impediments, people might utilize sober-minded approaches, for example, feast arranging, bunch cooking, and practical buying systems, to upgrade dinner readiness and ensure the accessibility of sustaining food sources. Moreover, developing straightforward discourse with close associates, family members, and colleagues in regards to one's dietary tendencies and goals can work with the obtaining of compassion and consolation from valued ones, consequently aiding the upkeep of healthy eating schedules notwithstanding outside impacts.

Moreover, the presence of inner variables including pressure, profound eating, and food desires can introduce significant deterrents to the support of good dieting designs. Integrating food for comfort or redirection to adapt to gloomy feelings like fatigue, distress, or nervousness can possibly crash even the most kindhearted dietary expectations. To go up against profound eating, people might pick to develop elective survival strategies, including care, stress management procedures, and cooperation in help gatherings or meetings with emotional wellbeing experts. Through the improvement of upgraded mindfulness and flexibility, people can lay out more wellbeing cognizant systems for overseeing pressure and filling their bodies, accordingly weaning themselves from reliance on nourishment for comfort.

Physiological elements, including bigotries, sensitivities, and ailments, may likewise present particular obstructions to the upkeep of good dieting rehearsals. Dietary limitations can make it challenging for people to find fitting food choices and explore social circumstances in which facilities may not be promptly accessible. To handle these obstructions, people might want to team up intimately with nutritionists, enlisted dietitians, or medical care experts to figure out individualized dietary systems that fulfill their nourishing prerequisites while likewise representing any dietary constraints or ailments. By investigating elective recipes, substituting fixings, or using specific food items, people who stick to dietary limitations can see the value in a different and satisfying eating regimen as well as advance their general wellbeing and prosperity.

On a very basic level, the capacity to overcome hindrances and difficulties chasing supporting sustaining schedules requires guts, flexibility, and preparation to change winning circumstances. Through the most common way of perceiving potential obstructions, planning viable strategies to conquer them, and seeking after help from dependable assets, people can capably move through the complexities of the dietary excursion with confidence and tastefulness. As our examination continues, may we hold onto the event to overcome hindrances and difficulties that obstruct the support of sustaining schedules, discerning of the way that conquering each such test propels us steadily towards further developed wellbeing and, by and large, health.

The Improvement of Flexibility and Versatility

In the unique domain of presence, it is basic to foster characteristics of flexibility and versatility to conquer difficulties and stay undaunted in our interests, for example, through the support of good dieting designs. This finishing-up portion digs into the meaning of versatility and flexibility in actually exploring the difficulties and changes of the dietary journey. Moreover, it gives commonsense ways to deal with developing these qualities inside.

Flexibility, which is as often as possible characterized as the ability to recuperate from difficulties, is a significant property with regards to laying out and getting through solid schedules. Versatile people can support an uplifting outlook, continue in the undertaking to accomplish their targets, and emerge from difficulty more braced and strong than previously. Creating survival techniques, sustaining a hopeful standpoint, and building a strong emotionally supportive network of family, companions, and local area individuals who can offer direction and consolation during misfortune are parts of encouraging versatility.

Conversely, flexibility relates to the ability to change one's methodology in light of developing circumstances and environmental factors. Versatility is extremely critical in the field of nourishment to effectively explore the various snags and disturbances that might happen, remembering modifications for way of life and dietary inclinations, unexpected conditions like illness or travel, and monetary constraints. Versatile individuals are equipped to change their dietary plans and schedules in an adaptable way to accommodate new conditions while staying focused on their principal wellbeing targets and values.

To foster strength and versatility during the course of dietary change, people might use a range of even-minded approaches and outlook changes. One such methodology is to reevaluate hindrances as learning and improvement open doors. Individuals can move toward mishaps and hindrances with a disposition of request and responsiveness, looking for illustrations and experiences that can direct their future activities and choices instead of seeing them as unrealistic obstructions.

Moreover, the foundation of taking care of oneself and the prioritization of mental and profound wellbeing are principal components in the improvement of strength and flexibility. Taking part in exercises that cultivate self-empathy, unwinding, and stress reduction, for example, journaling, yoga, or care contemplation, can help individuals create profound versatility and defeat life's hindrances all the more.

Besides, the development of flexibility and versatility is dependent upon the upkeep of a development mindset, which is characterized as a conviction in one's ability to obtain information and create through experience. By seeing difficulties as opportunities for self-improvement, individuals can develop a sense of skill and faith in their own capacity to overcome boundaries and achieve their goals.

Moreover, developing social associations with people who share comparable interests and objectives can offer critical inspiration, backing, and obligation all through the dietary journey. Looking for friendship and fortitude, whether it be through joining support gatherings, partaking in web-based networks, or creating amigo frameworks with companions or family, can help people overcome impediments and keep up with their devotion to their wellbeing goals.

On a very basic level, the improvement of flexibility and versatility is basic for the advancement and food of getting through dietary practices in the midst of the undeniable variances of presence. People can improve their strength and versatility all through their dietary process by developing survival techniques, advancing good faith, taking care of themselves as vital, keeping a development outlook, and mentioning support from others. As we attend a nearby examination, may we hold onto the event to cultivate strength and versatility in our own lives, perceiving that these traits will be profitable as we continue looking for further developed wellbeing and generally government assistance.

| 13 |

Chapter 13: Conclusion

Basically Revised Action Items

In the last snapshots of our investigation of "Brilliant Years, Brilliant Plates: Eating Great After 50," we actually must pause to consider the main acknowledgement and examples that have been conferred. Throughout this scholarly work, we have inspected the complicated relationship between our sustenance and sound maturing, uncovering the strategies and essentials that can empower us to thrive during our later years. At this point, we compactly sum up the central bits of knowledge, consolidating the voluminous data into functional rules that perusers might coordinate into their everyday schedules to accomplish perseverance through prosperity and energy.

It is apparent that sustenance essentially impacts the advancement of life span and the improvement of personal satisfaction during the maturing system. Through the reception of careful eating rehearses, the utilization of entire food sources, and the readiness of even feasts, people can support their wellbeing, reinforce their bodies, and decrease the probability of creating persistent sicknesses that every now and again manifest in advanced age. Through an assessment of dietary examples like the Mediterranean eating regimen and an appreciation for the meaning of supplements like fiber, vitamin D, and calcium, we have revealed the central parts of a nutritious eating regimen that can advance ideal wellbeing and prosperity in advanced age.

Furthermore, we have underscored the meaning of focusing on equilibrium, assortment, and delight while embracing a feasible way to deal with fortifying eating. Rather than depending on prohibitive eating regimens or moment cures, individuals have the choice to foster a lifestyle that revolves around devouring supplement-rich food varieties that give ideal substantial wellbeing while likewise getting delight from feasting and food. By carrying out feast arranging, group planning, and careful eating rehearses, it is feasible to lay out a dietary routine that supports the body as well as advances profound, physical, and otherworldly prosperity, in this way developing a condition of wellbeing that reaches beyond the bounds of the eating region.

Besides, we have analyzed the significance of versatility and flexibility in successfully dealing with the challenges and obstructions that might appear during the most common way of embracing another eating regimen. By advancing the improvement of a development outlook, sharpening methods for dealing with stress, and looking for help from others, individuals can overcome hindrances, keep up with their commitment to wellbeing goals, and emerge more hearty and versatile than they were beforehand. Concerning dealing with close-to-home eating, parties, and feasting out, we have outfitted perusers with the fundamental assets and strategies to proficiently explore the complexities of the contemporary food scene with affirmation and refinement.

Generally, the major knowledge gathered from our investigation of "Brilliant Years, Brilliant Plates" is that maturing in a sound way is an opportunity for each person, regardless of age or circumstance. Through the reception of sustaining dietary works, developing care, and creating flexibility, it is feasible to embrace the limit with regards to upgraded wellbeing, imperativeness, and by and large prosperity all through one's brilliant years and then some. As we finish up this volume, may we convey forward the information and understandings gained, starting a new stage described by prosperity, satisfaction, and outcome in the years to come.

Offering Inspiration and Support

In closing the last part of "Brilliant Years, Brilliant Plates: Eating Great After 50," we genuinely should give our perusers an expression of motivation and support. Despite the fact that there might be times when it appears to be overpowering to start an excursion towards focusing on wellbeing through nourishment during our brilliant years, it is important to remember that each steady measure towards further developed wellbeing is a positive step.

We might want to start by underlining to our perusers that taking on better dietary and lifestyle choices is unendingly conceivable. Regardless of one's ongoing stage, whether setting out on the investigation of good dieting or an accomplished specialist, each undertaking towards improving one's nourishment and, by and large, prosperity is critical and merits reward.

We emphatically suggest that you leave on your dietary journey with a mentality of curiosity, openness, and self-sympathy. Rather than seeking after flawlessness or respecting feelings of responsibility or embarrassment when one goes astray from the expected way, one ought to embrace the learning and improvement process that goes with the reception of better choices. Celebrate your achievements, independent of their greatness, and exercise self-empathy when faced with snags or relapses that unfold during your excursion.

Furthermore, we might want to highlight the huge impact that setting wellbeing as a first concern through legitimate nourishment can have on one's general personal satisfaction. Taking on careful eating rehearses and devouring nutritious, supplement-rich food sources can prompt various positive medical advantages, including expanded energy, an upgraded temperament, improved mental capability, and a diminished risk of creating constant sicknesses. Your dietary choices have the ability to impact the course of your wellbeing and empower you to have an existence overflowing with imperativeness, bliss, and significance.

At long last, we ask you to remember that you are not navigating this way alone. A wealth of assets and backing are available to help people all through their excursion, including partners, relatives, medical care experts, and online networks. At the point when you require direction, support, or responsibility, go ahead and carry it out. We can commonly help each other in our brilliant years to accomplish our wellbeing targets and carry on with our most ideal lives.

As you finish up this book and start the ensuing period of your journey, remember that you have the ability to impact your wellbeing and prosperity essentially. Stay devoted to focusing on your wellbeing through appropriate sustenance, keep up with strength when faced with hindrances, and stay motivated by the prospect of the dynamic and satisfying future that lies ahead. Albeit the excursion might contain surprising difficulties, it is feasible to accomplish one's wellbeing targets and prosper in advanced age with constancy, inspiration, and responsibility.

Offering valuable assets

As we draw to a close on our assessment of "Brilliant Years, Brilliant Plates: Eating Great After 50," it is obvious that the quest for ideal wellbeing and health is a persistent undertaking requiring consistent revelation and advancing all through one's lifetime. To work with the continuous examination of the subjects tended to in this book, we have arranged a specification of advantageous materials that can be used for extra consideration and exploration.

It is exceptionally prudent to start by finding believable sites, books, and online assets that are explicitly centered around the subject of nourishment and solid maturing. To advance wellbeing and prosperity in advanced age, definitive sites, remembering those of the Public Establishment for Maturing, the American Heart Association, and the Foundation of Sustenance and Dietetics, give an overflow of viable counsel and proof-based information. Moreover, academic works including "How Not to Bite the Dust" by Dr. Michael Greger and "The Blue Zones" by Dan Buettner offer huge commitments by analyzing the dietary and way of life practices of societies and people who have achieved astounding life spans and essentialness.

Also, for those looking to build their insight and appreciation of nourishment and sound maturing, webcasts and narratives can act as exceptional assets of information and motivation. As to wellbeing and prosperity, digital broadcasts, for example, "Nourishment Diva" and "The Plant Evidence Webcast," dig into a broad exhibit of subjects. Conversely, narratives like "Forks Over Blades" and "Food Matters" present enticing contentions concerning the capability of plant-based diets to deflect and turn around persistent illnesses.

Besides chasing after better wellbeing, online networks and care groups might offer altogether gainful consolation, inspiration, and responsibility. Gatherings like those tracked down on Reddit's r/nourishment and r/HealthyFood people groups, MyFitnessPal, and SparkPeople give valuable open doors to clients to speak with peers who share comparable interests, share individual encounters, and acquire direction and backing from other people who are going through similar cycles.

Moreover, we advocate for perusers to research local area-based encouraging groups of people and neighborhood assets, including senior focuses, health workshops, and cooking classes. These open doors offer huge possibilities for obtaining information, forming associations with similar people, and taking part in friendly exercises.

We finish up by underscoring that the quest for ideal wellbeing and prosperity is a single and customized try, without any trace of a generally relevant technique. Proceed with your excursion toward solid maturing by looking through your tenable assets, staying open to groundbreaking thoughts and viewpoints, and laying out associations with other people who share your objectives and values. Thusly, you can develop, learn, and succeed. We broaden our true wishes for your continuous success and fulfillment as you dive into the valuable materials, making progress toward further developed wellbeing, imperativeness, and by and large prosperity all through your brilliant years and then some.

Celebrating Advances and Accomplishments

As the "Brilliant Years, Brilliant Plates: Eating Great After 50" journey approaches, it is essential to stop and recognize the progressions and achievements that have been accomplished all through. Each step made toward setting wellbeing as a first concern through sustenance comprises an imperative achievement meriting recognition and celebration.

In the first place, we broaden our genuine deference for the courage and commitment displayed by our perusers as they begin their quest for further developed wellbeing and, generally, health. You have previously shown an eagerness to put resources into yourself and your future by moving toward focusing on wellbeing, in spite of the trouble of changing your way of life and sustenance.

Likewise, we recognize the gradual increases and huge dates that outperformed in the meantime. Positive activities like coordinating a more noteworthy assortment of foods grown from the ground into one's eating regimen, exploring different avenues regarding another recipe, and choosing feasts with goals all contribute to the steady accomplishment of one's wellbeing targets. By perceiving and remembering these victories, one reinforces their drive and devotion to progressing.

Moreover, we wish to recognize the great impacts that putting wellbeing as a first concern by means of sustenance has had on your all-encompassing government assistance. You might have noticed upgrades in your state of mind, energy levels, or rest quality; you might have additionally experienced unmistakable medical advantages, like weight reduction, irritation decrease, or improved glucose guidelines. No matter what the positive changes that have happened, they act as proof of the extraordinary capability of a nutritious eating regimen for one's wellbeing and imperativeness.

Moreover, we honor the persistence and resolve that our perusers show when faced with deterrents and mishaps all through their excursion. The way to further develop wellbeing isn't without difficulties, and snapshots of vulnerability may infrequently demonstrate how hard it is to conquer. By and by, through keeping up with strength, focus on goals, and immovability in regards to one's wellbeing, you have displayed a flawless dedication to one's general government assistance that warrants tribute.

We finish up by recognizing the actual excursion—the victories and disappointments, the hindrances and improvements, the occasions of self-awareness and disclosure. Each experience, regardless of its temperament (positive or pessimistic), had an impact on your continuous advancement towards further developed wellbeing and prosperity, cultivating your self-improvement and improvement. Realizing that we all who have gone with you on this journey uphold, energize, and celebrate you as you recognize your accomplishments and progress. All the best for your continued essentialness, wellbeing, and satisfaction in your brilliant years!

Prospecting the Future with Positive Thinking and Trust

As we draw near on our scholarly investigation of "Brilliant Years, Brilliant Plates: Eating Great After 50," we enthusiastically expect and ponder the impending years. Through the gathering of information, bits of knowledge, and encounters, we have been supplied with the vital assets and instruments to support our obligation to advance our wellbeing by means of nourishment soon.

Regardless of anything else, we approach the future with good faith, insightful of the way that consistently offers a new opportunity to lay out great choices that advance our physical and mental government assistance. Each activity we attempt, including choosing food sources that are plentiful in supplements, partaking in actual work, developing social associations, and rehearsing care, adds to our general prosperity and essentialness.

Besides, we keep an uplifting perspective on the future, recognizing the significant effect that a nutritious eating routine can have on further developing our general prosperity and cultivating solid maturing. By earnestly taking on the standards and systems portrayed in this artistic work, we can deftly cross the hindrances and possibilities of the maturing system while keeping a cool head, respect, and grit. In doing so, we will wager upon a future overflowing with imperativeness, wellbeing, and satisfaction.

Besides, realizing that we are in good company on this journey, we expect the future with affirmation. We are lucky to have the help of our networks, medical care suppliers, and friends and family, all of whom are there to empower, provide guidance, and help us when vital. We can stay inspired, defeat impediments, and stay focused on our well-being goals by developing a strong, emotionally supportive network and encircling ourselves with positive impacts.

As we think about the future, we are loaded up with appreciation for the joint undertaking we have finished hitherto and the possibilities that lie ahead. As we continue onward with certainty, may we bestow the information and understandings obtained from our examination, perceiving that each step we attempt brings us closer to a presence overflowing with prosperity, happiness, and wellbeing. Commencement to the brilliant years with reestablished idealism, confidence, and a solid internal compass!

Milton Keynes UK
Ingram Content Group UK Ltd.
UKHW050438280324
440101UK00016B/1158